I0616193

A PATH OF SORROWS

SPECIAL EDITION

PHILLIP BRESCIA

Copyright © 2025 by Phillip Brescia
All rights reserved.
ISBN: 979-8-89324-644-5

No part of this book may be reproduced, stored in a retrieval system, or transmitted in any form or by any means—electronic, mechanical, photocopying, recording, or otherwise—without prior written permission of the publisher, except for brief quotations used in reviews or articles.

The opinions expressed by the Author are not necessarily those held by the Publishers.

The information contained within this book is strictly for informational purposes. The material may include information, products, or services by third parties. As such, the Author and Publisher do not assume responsibility or liability for any third-party material or opinions. The publisher is not responsible for websites (or their content) that are not owned by the publisher. Readers are advised to do their own due diligence when it comes to making decisions.

Published by Franklin Publishers
Printed in the United States of America

For permissions, inquiries, or additional copies, contact:
Franklin Publishers
www.franklinpublishers.com

Table of Contents

PREFACE

———•●•———

There are many emotional states common to the human condition, and we experience so many of them to some degree throughout our lives. Positive emotions like love, happiness, joy, and excitement seem to enter our lives with a big fat, happy "hello" from us. They are the welcome surprises in life, and they accompany the moments we most cherish. These are the ones we want to hang on to and reminisce about from time to time. When the opportunity arises to share these stories, we are all too eager to recount, even momentarily, these happy and joyous occasions.

However, in this all-too-dualistic world, our lives are also filled with the negative. We can so easily find ourselves swimming in a pool of doubt, fear, anxiety, and sorrow. Unlike the positive emotions, whose surfaces seem so smooth, difficult to hold on to, and downright slippery, the sorrowful side of life is coarse and filled with barbs that attach themselves to our very being. They can cling to us for days, months, years, and for some of us, a lifetime. They weave themselves into our souls' tapestry and remain with us forever in some cases. There are certain events in human life that are tragic. No matter how much time passes, you never forget them—and you never forget the emotions that surround them. In time, with help, patience, and love, we can build a buffer around them to soften their effect on us and our psyches.

There are those who deal effectively with negative emotions, and then there are the rest of us. I don't understand why some of us seem predestined for the negative and others seem to have an excellent grasp of the positive. My sorrows have shadowed me since childhood. In the 1970s and 1980s, no one spoke of depression. "Cries for help" were dealt with by giving a brisk slap on the back followed by an encouraging phrase, such as, "Tomorrow will be a better day, you'll see." The reality is that tomorrow is not always a better day, but we desperately cling to the hope that it will be. I was not diagnosed with depression until my forties. I spent over three decades living in the darkness of the ever-present thought that, somehow, I didn't matter. I spent half a lifetime trying new things and failing. At the peak of this darkness I found myself separated from my family, working a job I hated, and realizing I had no real friends. My life was heading nowhere—at least not where I had hoped.

I moved my family from Maine to Florida so we could all have a better opportunity. A few years after I did so, the economy got tough, and I had to take a job in Colorado. The pay was great, but I found myself isolated from everything that mattered to me. I struggled with the high altitude. Every time I stood up too fast, I almost passed out. I was informed it was altitude sickness and that the answer was exercise. If I just got into better shape, my lungs would hold more air and raise the oxygen level in my blood. I was told that would solve the problem.

So, motivated by the desire to *not* fall face-first into the dirt at work, I got up the next day at 4:00 a.m. and headed to the gym. I was living in a hotel at the time, and they had one on the property, which was nice. I got on the treadmill and started a twenty-minute jog. In a few short minutes, I found myself breathing hard and sweating profusely. It had been a few years since I'd exercised. I needed something to focus on. I started with the weirdly textured wallpaper. I began to look for the repeating pattern, which took no time at all. Okay, I was six minutes into this workout, and I had a full-on bout of ADD. I needed something to take my mind off the sweating, the heavy breathing, and the overwhelming desire to get off the treadmill and go make myself a waffle. In a moment of desperation (and what I'm calling "divine inspiration"), I decided to pray the Rosary.

Looking down at the treadmill's display panel, which showed my pathetic pace and frightening heart rate, I saw I had fourteen minutes to go. So, I figured that fourteen minutes combined with a five-minute cooldown was enough time to pray one of the mysteries of the Rosary.

For my first prayer, I chose the sorrowful mysteries. I'm not sure why I did, but it just seemed like the thing to do. I had spent some time learning how to meditate. I'd read a book by Dr. Wayne Dyer years earlier about meditation. It was a practice I had picked up from him and others. I found it helpful to meditate every morning. It brought me peace and calmed my internal self. It was something I was out of practice with when I was sent to Colorado. But here on the treadmill, the idea of combining meditation, running, and praying the Rosary came to me, and I gave it a whirl.

On this inaugural run, I found myself in deep meditation. I struggled to get a decade of Hail Marys to silently run through my mind. I was almost immediately transported to Jesus' moment in the Garden of Gethsemane. I could see him in the greatest of detail, and at times, I was unsure if the heavy breaths I could hear were coming from me or from him. I could sense him sweating, and I felt the ground on which he was kneeling. I looked at his face in my meditation and saw profound sorrow. I was familiar with this level of sorrow. It was a plague that had haunted me my entire life. At that moment, I shared something with Jesus that I had never expected to share. It was as though, for the first time in my life, I realized he truly understood what I had been struggling with. I also understood, at that moment, that in my Christianity, I had been so quick to make Jesus God that I had forgotten he was simply a man as he endured his trials. He was a man who had been given a purpose and a task in life. He was just like me—just like the rest of us.

At this epiphanic moment, the treadmill stopped. I had become so caught up in the sight of Jesus kneeling and praying that I never got past the agony in the garden. I was so weighed down in an emotional cascade that I forgot about my cooldown. I walked out of the gym, made my way to my hotel room, and opened my computer. I sat there for the next hour, writing down what I had experienced. I was desperate to make some sense of it all.

I woke up the next morning at 4:00 a.m. and went back to the gym, hopped on the same treadmill, and gave it another go. My experience was similar, but this time, I made it to the end of the Rosary. Again, after the run, I immediately rushed back to my room to catalog the event. Every day I did this, there was something new and yet something so familiar. I could relate to Jesus' experiences and realized that what he experienced during these events was more human than divine.

As I wrote down the emotions I could identify with, I opened my heart and eyes to Jesus, the man. In the darkest recesses of his life, where sorrow, loneliness, doubt, fear, and pain converged, I discovered a path that led me to the very heart of the sorrowful mysteries of the Rosary, and on that journey, I found solace, understanding, and a profound connection with the anguish and pain that Jesus himself bore in those final hours of his life.

I found common ground with God. It was as though I had died with Christ on the cross and felt born again. A term I had not understood until I experienced it.

This book is my best attempt at sharing this experience with the world. It sat unfinished for years as my life took unexpected turns and twists. I was sitting in mass one day, listening to the priest give a homily based on an Old Testament reading. In this homily, Aaron and Hur had to hold up Moses' hands to God so the Israelites would win their fight against the Amalekite army. Every time Moses dropped his hands, the Amalekites got the better of the fight. Losing this war would mean the end of the Israelites as a people. So, everything that could be done to ensure victory was done. In a frozen moment during that homily, it all clicked for me. The Old Testament is about a group of people trying to relate to and understand their God. The New Testament is about a God trying to relate to and save his people. It is a true reflection of the real and the ideal.

I originally thought that this book was written only for myself. I can tell you I had no agenda when I wrote this book. I didn't create an outline, and I planned nothing ahead of time. I simply sat and recounted what I experienced during my meditation sessions. With a real effort to keep myself and my ideas out of the writing, I wrote without thought. I wrote with more emotion than intellect. That is most likely the reason it sat unedited for so long. I was afraid to change the story or affect it any way by sending it through an editing process. I was worried that I would inject too much of me and somehow alter the work in a negative fashion. But the idea of completing the book was never far from my mind, and after years of contemplation, I eventually convinced myself that this could be something special, so I completed it. It was not until my Lenten commitment of 2022, and thanks to the prompting of my wife, Veronica, that I decided it was time to sit down and finish what I had started. It was the right time. I was now in a place that was so far from the darkness that I had struggled with years earlier. I was finally at a place where the outcome was nowhere near as significant as actually sharing the message. I finally understood that sorrow could be a path to redemption. It was for Jesus, and I suspect it is for many of us, as well.

I have used this book many times as a Lenten reflection. Even though I wrote it, there are things that stand out to me differently each time I read it. Life is not stagnant; it's ever-changing, and as it changes, so do we. From year to year, as I read this book and reflect on the suffering of Jesus and the question of why he had to suffer, I end up realizing things about myself and my own personal growth. As I was writing it, and many times as I have read it, I was inspired to go to the Bible and read the passages that surround the events in the book. I search for the nuances in the text. I attempt to look past the stories as moments in history and endeavor to understand why the story was written and how to apply the meaning of it to my everyday life. I have come to understand that the Bible is not just filled with linear wisdom. There are layers to the messages, and the stories and parables have the great effect of meeting you where you are in life. The meaning and the blessings are endless, and they can reach you no matter what you are going through if you allow them to do so. This book is an outcome of just that, my willingness to let the message in the mysteries penetrate me. I encourage you to sit silently with Jesus and contemplate his sorrow as you make your way through the story. I am confident you will find a deep connection to him as you think about the times in your life when it seemed like there was no one to help you or that the pain you experienced was unbearable. These all-too-human emotions were shared by a poor and simple man from Bethlehem. A man who walked a sorrowful path that led to his death, resurrection, and ascension into heaven. This sorrowful path helped Jesus, the man, become what he was ultimately born to be, the King of kings. I hope that reflecting on the sorrows in this book helps you to understand your own struggles and aids you on your way to becoming all that God created you to be. Peace be with you.

Dedication

———◦•◦———

This book is dedicated to two of the most wonderful women I have ever known. The first is my wife Veronica, without whose help and constant encouragement this book would not exist. She is my constant source of inspiration and has the ability to keep me centered on what matters most. She is the love of my life.

The second woman is my sister Colleen. Since we were kids she has always been there for me. She is the embodiment of generosity and has the most loving of hearts. She is a beautiful person and I love her dearly.

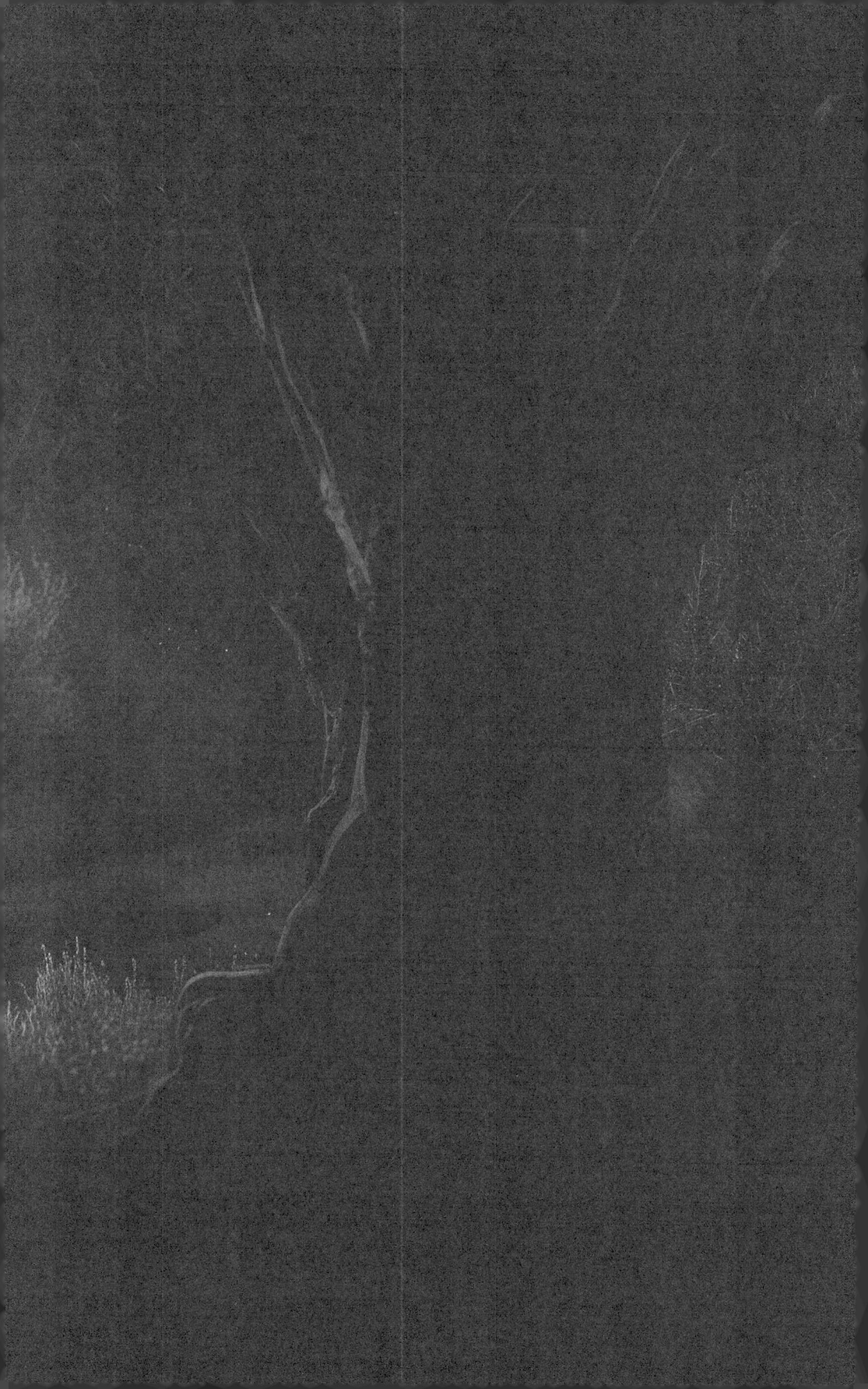

CHAPTER 1

Gethsemane

——•●•——

He gazed around the room lovingly, cherishing these final moments with his companions. The simple, unadorned room held an unspoken reverence, its sparse furnishings a testament to the humility in which they gathered. A table was set, and the guests had taken their places, reclining around it to share a meal together. As the sun set, a growing stillness filled the room; oil lamps were lit, their flickering light casting shadows that seemed to shift and breathe as if the walls themselves bore witness to the holiness of the hour. The shadows could not mirror the fellowship shared by the group; they could only cast their silent, dark images around the room. Yet in the stillness, an air of anticipation clung to the darkness as if the shadows themselves sensed the hour of their defeat was near. They seemed to make a final stand, amplifying the movements of the room's inhabitants, their flickering forms straining to be seen. Only Jesus took notice, his gaze quiet and watchful as he observed the shadows flicker and clash in a soundless struggle for attention.

The room was small for the number of inhabitants, and the mood was cheerful as a meal was shared by all. As the guests wrapped themselves in conversation, they could not have realized the weight or significance of the moment. It was obvious they did not. The meal was accompanied by a lively discussion. It was a familiar dialogue, which included the well-being of family and friends, complaints about the government, and their shared hopes and dreams for the future. None other than Jesus broke away from the intense discussions, which grew louder as each person raised their voice to be heard over the constant chatter and laughter that filled the small space. Only Jesus, who had quietly detached from the conversation, noticed the subtle shift in the room—the shadows lengthening, darkness edging closer. Yet how could the others understand what was to come? It would be some time before the events of this night would take shape in their hearts. Even though Jesus was in a room with his closest and most trusted companions, for the first time, he truly felt alone. The hour was drawing near, an hour he knew from the beginning was unavoidable. His path had always been clear, yet he sensed his human heart would soon face a test beyond anything ever known. This was the moment for which he knew he had been born. These men, with whom he shared so much love, could not understand his pain. They were blind to the significance of the hour, and Jesus understood it was meant to be so. He longed to reach out, to embrace them as brothers, but he knew he must prepare himself, and them for what lay ahead. He could speak of it, but what purpose would that serve? In time, all would be revealed, and so he remained silent, for this was his hour to fulfill his Father's will.

The sun had set, and Jesus had washed the feet of those who were loyal to him. In a profound act of compassion, he even washed the feet of the one who would betray him, a gesture meant to show the apostles the path toward the light. Through faith in God, forgiveness, and service to others, they were bound to the Holy One.

They reclined again at the table. He picked up the bread and gave thanks to the Father.

While they were eating, Jesus took bread, said the blessing, broke it, and giving it to his disciples said, "Take and eat; this is my body." Then he took a cup, gave thanks, and gave it to them, saying, "Drink from it, all of you, for this is my blood of the covenant, which will be shed on behalf of many for the forgiveness of sins."

—Matthew 26:26–28

What the Twelve did not know was this was the last time they would share a meal with him. Only Jesus understood the events that lay ahead, and he sensed that the hour was near. There was much preparation to do before he could carry out everything for which he had been born.

He took them out of the room, through the darkness, leading them to the Mount of Olives. Once there, he asked them to keep watch with him, trusting them with this solemn request.

As Jesus approached the Garden of Gethsemane, a profound grief welled within him—a sorrow unlike any he had ever known.

He took along Peter and the two sons of Zebedee, and began to feel sorrow and distress. Then he said to them, "My soul is sorrowful even to death. Remain here and keep watch with me."

—Matthew 26: 37–38

It was a cool night, and the wind blew gently through the trees. Their fragrance hit his nose and filled his mind with God's wonder. He fell to the ground in desperate prayer to the Father. The earth beneath him was cold and damp, yet he remained unmoved by its chill. He knew what he had to do, yet he also knew that no human heart could bear the weight of what lay before him. Though his life was divine, his heart was human, and it would be tested beyond mortal limits. He prayed to the Father for strength in this hour of need, his heart groaning with the grief of a parent mourning the loss of a child. This garden, once a place of solace and joy, had now become the ground upon which he would face one of his greatest tests. Almost immediately, a new depth of despair began to stir within him, unlike anything he had ever known.

It was a test of faith, a test of love, a test of compassion—but also an act of true charity. He was sent to save souls. He was sent to remove sin from the world. Jesus understood this, yet the thought of leaving his friends weighed heavily on his heart. They meant so much to him, and each day, their numbers grew, a testament to his Father's glory. Must it come to this? He wondered though he knew the answer. If he did not bear the sins of the world, who would? He knew it would bring unimaginable pain, sorrow, and agony—a sorrow beyond any ever endured by man or earthly creature. Jesus also knew that once he began this final journey, there would be no turning back. He would have to see it through to the very end. This night, he would undertake a journey beyond the bounds of heaven and earth, one that would pierce even the netherworld. It was a journey beyond what any human heart could endure or conceive. Not even Satan, from the deepest depths of hell, could summon pain of this magnitude. But Jesus, the beloved Son, fully aware of his mission, began to walk the long and lonely path of sin—a path he had never walked before.

His task, now before him, had started at the beginning of time. There, at the moment of creation of the heavens and the earth, he had stood, gazing upon the wonder and splendor of it all. He had admired it for its beauty and perfection. Jesus stopped and looked at the earth and knew what to expect, for this was not the first time he had been here. He witnessed the creation of man, and it was good. God was no longer alone, for he had a companion with whom to share his boundless love. Yet, man could not fully embrace God as a true companion. Adam was lonely, and in his love, God gave Adam a partner—Eve. But then, the serpent approached, and Eve seduced, tasted the forbidden fruit, and shared it with Adam. At that moment, Jesus shed a tear. This was where sin began, the moment it entered God's glorious creation.

His heart had never known sin before. It was heavy and burned from the inside out. It was almost sour in taste and made him feel as if he were going to be sick. He did not want it inside him. Its nature was foul, and it left him feeling cold and abandoned. He wanted to drop it like a hot stone but could not. What was more troubling was that he knew he would have to hold on to it tightly and guard it. Jesus felt like he had never before. To regain his composure, Jesus took a deep breath and slowly let it out; he knew what he had to do next.

Jesus looked forward to Cain and Abel. For the second time, he bore witness as Cain, overcome with jealous rage, struck down his brother. The cruelty and pain of this act seared his heart anew, and as Cain stood in the field, covered in his brother's blood, Jesus again wept. He gathered the weight of Cain's sin within himself, and it burned even more fiercely than the first. The burden of these sins set Jesus' heart on fire. This was no ordinary fire—it was not one of warmth or light. This was a raging inferno, a flame that seemed to consume everything in its path as if the fires of hell itself had ignited within him. Jesus knew this was only the beginning and that far more lay ahead. One by one, each soul appeared before Jesus, and he took into his heart the weight of their sins. Each sin intensified the sorrow within him, feeding a flame that now burned with an unrelenting heat. He carried this burden until he came to Noah. Though not without sin, Noah offered a small respite—a man who trusted deeply in God's will, faithful and committed. In Noah's trust, Jesus found a brief moment of relief, a strength that steadied him, even as he prepared to continue bearing the sins of the world.

From here, Jesus watched as the mighty flood wiped out the world, and man was given a fresh start. The sins of ancient man now gathered within him weighed on his heart like an anchor to his soul. But Jesus knew why he was on the earth, and he understood the task he was undertaking. He prayed to the Father for strength and continued, gathering sins from every age of history, for he would come to know them all. Along this path, he encountered people who brought him deep joy, like Abraham. Abraham's loyalty and devotion to God lifted Jesus' spirit, easing his heart as he took on the weight of sin. He knew that the hour of his own trial would come soon, and he pressed onward through the pain and suffering, all for the glory of the One who had sent him.

Jesus continued his journey through time. He watched as the Israelites crossed the Red Sea and wandered through the desert, only to become indignant when he saw them kneeling before the golden calf. In that moment, he felt his heart nearly burst. How could these chosen people so swiftly turn away from the God who had delivered them? He shared in Moses' anger as the commandments were shattered in the presence of their idolatry. He felt himself nearly losing control but knew he must remain focused on his love for all humanity. This was why he was doing this. An intense wound opened within him—one he had never known. How could those whom he and the Father loved above all else fail to love them in return? In his sorrow, Jesus felt profoundly alone, his face lowered to the ground. In that moment, he bore the weight of creation's anger, hatred, and greed—the very creation God had called his beloved.

As Jesus wrestled with the countless failures of humankind, he sensed a dark presence closing in around him. He knew it was evil, and this knowledge only deepened his resolve to press on. In a chilling whisper, the devil spoke into his ear, "No human heart can hold the sins of man. I know the depth of man's sin, for it is my domain." Jesus ignored the devil, prayed to the Father again for strength, then continued. The devil circled him, trying to divert his focus, but to no avail. Jesus pressed forward, undaunted, under the devil's watchful and relentless gaze.

Jesus continued to walk the path of sin with everyone who had ever lived. He knew man, and he knew the depth of man's sin. He felt this pain acutely and knew he had been born to bring salvation, to free humanity from sin through forgiveness. Here, in this garden, he would demonstrate to all people the meaning of submission to God's will and obedience to the Holy Spirit. In this place, he would stand against sin and lead his people to the Promised Land. Here, within Satan's dominion, he would conquer sin, for this was his divine purpose. The sins he bore were too numerous to count, each one a heavy burden, yet he continued forward. Though time seemed to stand still in these moments, he knew his time was limited, and so he pressed on, undaunted, enduring for the glory of the Father. Jesus watched as the temple of God was raised and then brought to ruin. He saw humanity moving blindly through their lives, entrenched in sin. For those who did not know God, the weight of their sins was heavy, but it did not pierce him in the same way. Yet for those who knew God—those who had received the Law, who understood what it meant to be just—their sins struck him like a blade. They knew better. They knew what it meant to be just. Had God not given them the Law to live by? Did he not give them what they asked for? Although he taught them how to live, they refused to listen to him. The sins of those who believed in God hit Jesus like a sword. They tore at his heart, each one a painful reminder of their knowledge and willful turning away. His heart, once pure and unsullied, grew heavy under the stain of these sins, burdened by the rejection of God's chosen people. With each sin, his heart bled anew, bearing the sorrow of a love unreturned.

Jesus witnessed the rise and fall of kings and kingdoms, a cycle marred by endless wars and bloodshed. None of this was godly. None of these actions seemed to be in God's will. Jesus watched as God gave kings to

Israel to protect them, only for them to lose faith in him. He watched as they were driven from their land, then later returned after bloodshed and battle. Jesus was with the soldiers, one by one, collecting the sins of warfare. The slaying of another person is a sin that left a mark on Jesus' heart. The giving and taking of life belonged to God alone, yet here, in the heat of battle, men claimed that power, reaching an unprecedented height of vanity. Kings of the earth would "play god," distributing death and judgment as they pleased, dictating the hour of another's end. But they could not create life—only destroy it. And yet, in their arrogance, they believed themselves in control. Jesus collected all the sins from those who were vain with some difficulty, for they neither feared nor revered the Lord. His purpose in this hour was not to judge but to collect what needed to be redeemed from the earth. This would pave the way for salvation, opening the gates to grace. This was why Jesus had come, why he would be crowned King of kings.

Jesus accumulated all of mankind's sins—until he finally witnessed his own birth. The weight of emotional pain and suffering had become nearly unbearable, and he looked to his disciples for solace, seeking comfort in their presence. He had gathered the sins of ages past, and with a quiet glance heavenward, he thanked God that this part of his burden was complete. Thousands of years of sins now rested within his human heart, each one his to bear. Though the pain and weight of these sins bore down heavily upon him, he felt a profound desire to share this first victory with those he loved. As he lifted himself from the ground for the first time, he felt the weight of his own human form as a burden. Never before had he been so aware of the heaviness of his earthly frame, and as he rose, his head spun. He steadied himself, drawing in a deep breath, and walked toward his disciples—only to find them asleep.

"So you could not keep watch with me for one hour? Watch and pray that you may not undergo the test. The spirit is willing, but the flesh is weak."

—Matthew 26:40–41

Jesus was hurt by their lack of spirit and faith. In that moment, he experienced a profound sense of abandonment, even by those dearest to him. How could they have fallen asleep at such a time? Could they not sense that he bore this burden for their sake? Frustration and disappointment clouded his thoughts, and he stood in silence, awaiting a response that would never come. Perhaps, he thought, they were simply not ready to be left on their own.

Jesus retreated again into the garden to pray.

He said, "Abba, Father, all things are possible to you. Take this cup away from me, but not what I will but what you will."

—Mark 14:36

Jesus asked the Father in heaven to save him from this journey. He wrestled with the thought that his disciples might not yet be ready to face the world alone. He held these thoughts close, allowing them only a moment's breath. He had gathered so many followers in such a short time; couldn't he remain just a little while longer? He wondered about the impact his continued ministry could bring: How many more of God's children might he save if given more time? How many more afflicted by leprosy could he heal, how many sick made well, how many blind granted sight? And all this would be done in God's name, his glory magnified. How many more would believe? This prayer was spoken by one who worried deeply for his children. How could he leave them now, knowing their unpreparedness, when they could not even keep watch with him for an hour?

Jesus knelt in silent prayer, but he did not receive an answer from the Father. He understood that his time had come and that seeking another path would be against God's will. Jesus, ever the obedient Son, took a steadying breath and resumed his task of gathering sins. His thoughts drifted back to his birth, to the glory of God-made flesh. He stopped to gaze upon his mother, and with a lifting of his spirit, he collected her love into his heart. Her love was the closest to the Father's that Jesus had ever encountered on the earth. His mother was a pillar of strength and grace. Jesus thought about his mother's devotion to God. When the angel appeared to her to announce his birth, she acclaimed: *"Behold, I am the handmaid of the Lord. May it be done to me according to your word"* (Luke 1:38). Jesus knew his mother's love, but at that moment, he understood it was not love alone that had led his mother to become so. It was her strength and faith that had made her the only choice to bear God's only Son. Her courage in surrendering to Yahweh's will, regardless of the cost, inspired Jesus to embrace the Father's will and continue his task. One day, he would honor her for this sacrifice, but for now, his focus remained on the journey ahead.

He found strength in his mother's grace and faith, a comfort as he faced the presence of Herod—a man who neither knew God nor wished to. This was the son of the ruler who had sought to kill him as an infant, the same man who had ordered the death of John the Baptist. Collecting Herod's sins was especially difficult; it was as though those who belonged to darkness clung stubbornly to their sins, resisting even the possibility of redemption. It was as if they didn't want Jesus to take them. They rejected both salvation and God. There were many like this, souls who used their free will to choose sin time and again, turning away from God's love and the gift of his precious Son. Herod's heart was bound to earthly power, his gaze fixed on worldly gain, indifferent to the eternal. Jesus leaned ever more heavily on the Father's boundless love and mercy, gathering the sins of those whose hearts resisted release, unwilling to loosen their grip on the darkness within.

Jesus then thought of John the Baptist. John was a man deeply in love with God, the servant of the Almighty. Jesus looked upon this man's righteous life with love and collected the sins of the man who had baptized him with water. It was then that Jesus heard a voice again. It was the devil. He whispered in Jesus' ear, "No human heart can endure the sins of such wicked generations."

Jesus, unmoved, ignored these words, his mind turning to the beginning of his public ministry and the forty days he had spent in the desert, fasting and preparing for his calling. It was there that the devil had first tried to tempt him, a moment that now seemed so distant. He looked back upon that time and remembered the trials he had endured there. But the pain and discomfort of a forty-day fast was nothing compared to this. Jesus had never known pain and sorrow like this. The devil always seemed to show up when Jesus was weakened, and Jesus had never been this weak before. He had not known sorrow this deep. He felt as though his heart would fall from his chest due to its weight or perhaps explode from the pressure. He took a deep breath and gathered his thoughts. It was God's will that he was here, so he let the will of God be done. Realizing Jesus' resolve, the devil retreated, fading back into the shadows.

Jesus then found himself by the familiar shore of the Sea of Galilee, the place where he had first encountered Peter, then known as Simon. He gathered Peter and Andrew into his heart, lifting the weight of their sins. One by one, he did the same for each of his disciples—even the one who, at that very moment, was betraying him. Judas's sin carried a weight that seemed to pierce the depths of mortal understanding. Jesus breathed heavily, his voice breaking as he cried, "Why?!?" How could he forgive the one who would deliver him to the chief priests? A profound wave of sorrow and anger stirred within his heart, knowing that because of this man, he would be torn from those he loved so completely. The intensity of it swelled, momentarily clouding his purpose, as the weight of betrayal pierced through him. Yet even in this anguish, he recalled his mission and the shortness of time. Though every part of him longed to stay with his beloved friends, he surrendered to the will of God.

Jesus wept from the pain of sin and the sorrow of leaving those he loved so dearly. The pain was sharp, a stabbing ache, as though a raw nerve had been exposed to the blade of betrayal. Who could fault him for wanting to turn away from Judas, the chief priests, and the elders? In this moment, they represented nothing but destruction and grief for the Son of God. A short distance away, the devil watched in satisfaction, reveling in the agony of God's beloved Son, laughing at the torment that mankind's sins brought upon him. Having rejected God, the devil had come to revel in sin, for it was the one thing not of God. Jesus had never known sin before. This act—taking on the sins of the world—was unlike anything he had ever experienced. Though he had forgiven sins, he had never gathered them into himself. But he knew he must take them all. It was God's will and the only path to salvation for humankind. No one could be left behind without the chance of redemption. And so, with a groan of deep resolve, he continued, gathering the sins of Judas, the members of the Sanhedrin, and the chief priest.

Jesus labored on with his task. As he moved from person to person collecting their sins, he found himself on a wild and emotional journey. His hands began to tremble, and a wave of nausea surged within him. A sharp pain formed behind his right eye, and he raised his hand to steady himself, hoping it might soon pass. But even in this agony, he continued, gathering into his heart the sins of those who plotted against him, those who would bring about his death. He would carry these sins with him now, bearing them fully for the remainder of his journey.

He also thought of people of remarkable faith whom he had met, like the centurion with a sick slave. He took immense pleasure and satisfaction in helping someone with such faith. The slave was healed, and he and all his family had devoted themselves to God. He thought, too, of his beloved friends—Mary, Martha, and Lazarus—and his heart softened. His mind lingered on that day he had called Lazarus from the tomb, breathing life back into his friend's body, a moment filled with profound love and hope. These memories reminded him of the light within the darkness, small comforts in the midst of his growing burden.

Now a man was ill, Lazarus from Bethany, the village of Mary and her sister Martha. Mary was the one who had anointed the Lord with perfumed oil and dried his feet with her hair; it was her brother Lazarus who was ill. So the sisters sent word to him, saying, "Master, the one you love is ill." When Jesus heard this he said, "This illness is not to end in death, but is for the glory of God, that the Son of God may be glorified through it." Now Jesus loved Martha and her sister and Lazarus. So when he heard that he was ill, he remained for two days in the place where he was. Then after this he said to his disciples, "Let us go back to Judea.". . . So then Jesus said to them clearly, "Lazarus has died. And I am glad for you that I was not there, that you may believe. Let us go to him.", , , When Jesus arrived, he found that Lazarus had already been in the tomb for four days. Now Bethany was near Jerusalem, only about two miles away. And many of the Jews had come to Martha and Mary to comfort them about their brother. When Martha heard that Jesus was coming, she went to meet him; but Mary sat at home. Martha said to Jesus, "Lord, if you had been here, my brother would not have died. Even now I know that whatever you ask of God, God will give you." Jesus said to her, "Your brother will rise." Martha said to him, "I know he will rise, in the resurrection on the last day." Jesus told her, "I am the resurrection and the life; whoever believes in me, even if he dies, will live, and everyone who lives and believes in me will never die. Do you believe this?" She said to him, "Yes, Lord. I have come to believe that you are the Messiah, the Son of God, the one who is coming into the world." . . .

When Mary came to where Jesus was and saw him, she fell at his feet and said to him, "Lord, if you had been here, my brother would not have died." When Jesus saw her weeping and the Jews who had come with her weeping, he became perturbed and deeply troubled, and said, "Where have you laid him?" They said to him, "Sir, come and see." And Jesus wept. So the Jews said, "See how he loved him." But some of them said, "Could not the one who opened the eyes of the blind man have done something so that this man would not have died?"

So Jesus, perturbed again, came to the tomb. It was a cave, and a stone lay across it. Jesus said, "Take away the stone." Martha, the dead man's sister, said to him, "Lord, by now there will be a stench; he has been dead for four days." Jesus said to her, "Did I not tell you that if you believe you will see the glory of God?" So they took away the stone. And Jesus raised his eyes and said, "Father, I thank you for hearing me. I know that you always hear me; but because of the crowd here I have said this, that they may believe that you sent me." And when he had said this, he cried out in a loud voice, "Lazarus, come out!" The dead man came out, tied hand and foot with burial bands, and his face wrapped in a cloth. So Jesus said to them, "Untie him and let him go."

—John 11:1–7, 14–15, 17–27, 32–44

Jesus' heart grew heavy as he thought of those he loved, each memory deepening the sorrow within him. The thought of Mary's anointing, a gesture preparing him for what lay ahead, was vivid in his mind. He understood that death was drawing near, and like the day he had called Lazarus forth from the tomb, he lifted his eyes to God in prayer, his voice filled with gratitude and sorrow. "I know you are always with me," he prayed, "but my heart is heavy and sorrowful. Even so, may your will be done." Though he had fully surrendered to the Father's will, the thought of leaving those he cherished most brought a deep ache to his spirit. His love for the Father pulled him forward, yet his heart longed to remain with his beloved friends, and this conflict pressed upon him with a relentless weight. He wept anew as he gathered the sins of those closest to him. These very souls who had brought him strength through this agonizing task were now also the source of profound pain. And yet, he pressed on, carrying both the burden of their sins and the immeasurable love he held for each one.

He collected the sins of all the children, these innocent and tender souls whom he cherished so much. With each one, he felt a tear slip down, placing their sins carefully in a special place within his heart. His thoughts drifted to life's simple beauties, and he knew he would miss the sounds of children laughing, their pure voices carrying joy through the air. They were the purest souls on earth, unburdened by the judgments of the world. Each child reminded him of the angels in heaven, living to please the Father through love alone. Like the angels, these children loved openly and eagerly, longing only to be loved in return, with hearts untouched by malice or fear. Their eyes were still innocent. Even though they had original sin, they still had God's wonder and were guiltless, like Adam and Eve were at the beginning. They had not yet tasted the fruit of knowledge of good and evil and had not yet been banned from the Garden of Eden. Jesus loved the children and would miss them beyond measure. As he gathered the sins of the young, he found himself smiling, imagining kissing each one on the cheek. He prayed they would grow up to be as God-fearing and loving as they were now, carrying that same pure light within them.

Once more, his thoughts traveled to his disciples. They, too, were like children, vulnerable and in need of guidance. He knew they were not yet ready to walk this path alone, yet they were the ones he would soon have to leave behind. With the sins of the present gathered, he looked toward them, longing to return to their side.

Then he returned once more and found them asleep, for they could not keep their eyes open. He left them and withdrew again and prayed a third time.

—Matthew 26:43–44

"My Father, if it is possible, let this cup pass from me, but not as I will—as you will." Jesus was filled with sorrow beyond sorrows. Those he loved most slept on, and an overwhelming sense of solitude pressed upon him. He no longer felt the earlier sting of anger but instead a quiet acceptance, realizing his hour had truly come and that he alone would face the coming darkness. The weight of this solitude grounded him and forced him to see the reality of his future. For the first time in his life, he was truly alone. His heart broke with that thought, and he wondered how much he would have to endure before this was over. The sins of the world now gathered within him, pushing against his heart, straining as if to break free like a creature caged. His pain was not only emotional but also physical. The greatest challenge of the night was ahead of him. He was not sure he had the strength to go through with it. He would have to collect the sins of the world for future generations. Jesus knew mankind would become even more wicked and perverse in the future. He could feel the darkness threatening to take root, and he saw how, in time, sin would reach unimaginable depths. Yet, even in this grim knowledge, he gathered himself, determined to bear it all for the sake of those he loved.

The devil, who was still present in the garden, smiled. He knew what Jesus was thinking and what he had to do. The pain Jesus had felt thus far was only a shadow of what lay ahead, and the devil delighted in that knowledge. "No human heart can hold the sins of mankind," he whispered, his voice laced with smug confidence, "nor can one man endure the price that must be paid." He paused, his gaze fixed on Jesus' sorrowful eyes, and then hissed, "Release yourself from this burden. Let them go." Jesus met the devil's gaze, his face steady and resolute, before turning away, unmoved, and continued the task that lay before him.

Jesus looked into the future. He was glad to see his ministry would reach all corners of the earth. He was glad to witness the billions of people who would believe in God the Father. However, he also observed the hold the devil would place on man. He started to weep again at the sight of the destruction of the temple and the driving out of the Jews from Israel. He witnessed epic battles in numbers never seen before. It was as though the larger the earth's population grew, the larger the armies would become and the larger the evil that would spread. He saw the Roman Empire grow and the countless number of lives lost to meaningless violence. He saw how greed would corrupt rulers, enslaving not only individuals but entire nations under the weight of power and avarice. These visions flashed through his mind like lightning and bore down upon his soul with unbearable force. He watched as the years played out, and innocence was lost earlier and earlier in life. He felt the agony of those tortured in his name, the flames of those unjustly burned at the stake. Every injustice, every act of cruelty pierced his spirit. He lay on the ground, his body trembling with a force beyond his control, feeling as though a fire blazed within the very core of his being, threatening to consume him entirely. The pain in his chest pounded relentlessly, each beat like the echo of a man trapped within the confines of a coffin, desperately seeking escape. The pain was so severe in his head, he was sure it would split apart. He became exhausted and overwhelmed. The few lights he could see in the distance became fuzzy and out of focus. His head spun out of control. He did not know where he was anymore, and he was confident he would pass out soon. Yet, even in this extreme stress, his heart remained steady in its devotion. As an obedient son, he raised a silent plea to his Father for strength. No suffering, no depth of despair, would keep him from fulfilling the purpose for which he had come. He would endure it all, no matter the cost.

In his hour of greatest need, the Father, ever compassionate, sent an angel from heaven to strengthen his beloved Son. The angel descended in a radiant glow and, with a single command, drove the devil back into the shadows, ending the torment that darkness had brought. The angel brought the power of God to Jesus in the form of white light. The angel picked up Jesus' head, laid it on his lap, and began to pray and sing. A dim light from above rested on the Son of Man, and as the melody wrapped around him, Jesus felt his breath calm, the weight upon his chest easing. The angel's presence reminded him that his Father would remain with him throughout this journey, a steady strength that nothing could diminish. Reassured and comforted, Jesus found within himself the courage to continue, to face the sins of the future with renewed resolve.

In his mind, Jesus beheld the rise and fall of the Roman emperors, their sins darkening his spirit as he gathered the weight of their wickedness. He watched as these rulers, consumed by power, unleashed persecution upon those faithful to him and to the Father. He watched person after person suffer and die because they followed Jesus and loved the Father. His heart ached intensified as he foresaw the fates of his beloved disciples, each one meeting their end in his name. This pain was beyond any he had known; it shook him to the core. Jesus again began to breathe heavy and become dizzy. The angel of the Lord felt his distress and continued to hold his head and comfort him. However, Jesus did find moments of joy in the darkness of the abyss of sin. He saw his church growing, and the numbers of faithful people multiply greatly. With tenderness, he welcomed them into his heart, gathering even their sins, knowing that they, too, would walk in his love. The frailty of his human self became ever more apparent, the weight of sin pressing down upon him with relentless force. This was especially true for those who thrived on greed and war.

As he looked further into the future, he saw that mankind was becoming more efficient at killing. Even though there were those who worked every day for the glory of God, there were also those who worked for the destruction of others. Jesus saw how people treated each other and how perverse some would become. Jesus, at times, did not want to continue. The burden was now so heavy that he could barely lift his head, even with the angel's help. He was sure he would be lying face-down on the ground if it were not for his support. He was tired to the point of exhaustion. The thoughts of so many lost souls and the amount of sin in the world seemed to fill his mind to the point of overflowing. His pure heart, once a vessel of boundless love, now struggled under the strain of humanity's darkest evils. It puzzled him how it hadn't shattered from the immense weight he carried, for it was no longer just a fragment of sin but the totality of all sin—every cruelty, every betrayal, all the darkness that had ever existed, and all that was yet to come.

Just as Jesus thought he could bear no more, he was confronted with a vision of Adolf Hitler, a man whose actions would be responsible for the deaths of millions of God's chosen people. The scale of devastation, the depth of hatred and cruelty, sent a cry from his soul heavenward. He watched in horror as one person after another justified the atrocities unfolding, each justification like a blade turned within him. Millions perished, and countless others were complicit in their silence or support of this one man's twisted vision. The sins of Sodom and Gomorrah paled in comparison to what he saw now. Again, Jesus' spirit cried out in agony.

It was as if someone had tied a millstone around his neck and thrown him into the sea. He was drowning under the weight of it all and could barely breathe. He was so exhausted from this work. How full his heart was with sin. How full his soul was with sorrow. How much more could he endure? But because he loved us—each of us—and because he loved the Father, he could not leave any soul behind, no matter the cost.

Jesus paused for a moment and focused solely on his heavenly Father. He took a moment to forget what he was doing, to simply bask in the glory of God. This had always helped Jesus before in his life, and in these hours of desperate need, he could think of nothing else that would help him endure this horrific episode. So, by and through the grace of God, and with the help of the angel that was comforting him, he pressed on, collecting the sins of the world and finding a place in his heart for them. He collected the evil sins of those who would be known to man as thieves and murderers. He also collected from those who would become known as saints. Their goodness shone as a light within the darkness of his burden, each act of kindness, humility, and sacrifice a testament to the strength of the human spirit. Some of these saints would be honored by the church, but most would remain nameless, their virtues seen and cherished only by God and those they touched.

Jesus continued to gather the sins of the world, stretching forward through the ages to the modern day. He witnessed the creation of weapons with unimaginable power, tools crafted not to heal but to destroy. The sorrow within him grew unbearable, and he felt as though all of creation wept with him, mourning a future where humanity had turned its ingenuity to devastation. The depths of pain he felt at seeing this drove him to the brink; how deeply it grieved him to know the endless hours, the precious energy spent not on love or compassion but on tools of warfare. His heart ached as he watched lives thrown away through addiction, as he saw millions of unborn lives taken. The vast separation of humanity was laid bare before him, each soul straying further from the unity they were created for. He knew his church would grow to include billions of people but that it could not make right all that was against God in the world. With time slipping away, he labored on, each moment a fierce struggle as he knelt, pouring his strength into lifting the world closer to heaven as though he might somehow make it easier for each soul to find salvation. The strain was so immense that his body began to tremble, and his sweat turned to drops of blood, each one bearing witness to the unfathomable depth of his sacrifice.

The angel, now weeping openly, felt his heart breaking for the beloved Son of God. With tenderness, he lifted Jesus' head from the ground, pulling him close and holding him tightly as if to shield him from the burden he bore. Looking heavenward in silent prayer, the angel's face shone with grief and devotion as he pleaded for strength to be given to the one he held in his embrace. As the angel looked up toward heaven in prayer, a dim light shone on Jesus' head. He felt Jesus' pain and knew he desperately needed the Father's help, which he lovingly gave. The Father's presence surrounded him, filling the air with peace and a love beyond words. Jesus was now more at ease, and his breathing settled down as the light grew in intensity. The angel remained by his side, unwavering, his arms a source of comfort, his presence a quiet promise that he would not leave until the journey was complete. Jesus continued to gather the sins of the world into the distant future. He saw that the continued struggle between righteousness and evil, faith and control, and light and dark would go on for quite some time. Visions of the centuries to come flooded his mind, each image blurring into the next, a cascade of lives and choices too swift to hold individually. The enormity of it was staggering, and he no longer had time to pause or ponder the weight of each sin he took upon himself. Humanity's numbers had grown vast, and the sheer scope of it all demanded the intervention of God's glory, channeling every sorrow, every failure, every act of defiance into him like iron drawn to a magnet. Each sin burned within him like a scorching fire, stabbing at his soul with a searing heat that left him gasping. His strength faltered; his body no longer able to bear the weight alone. He collapsed once more, his face pressed to the ground as if the very earth sought to consume him under the weight of all he bore. Yet, even in this moment of weakness, his spirit held fast, determined to endure every agony for the sake of those he loved. At this point, Jesus felt he would have to stop out of pain and agony, but then, in the distance, he saw a great light. He recognized that bright and warm light beam. It was his Second Coming to the earth. Jesus had made it to the end.

Just as the pain became nearly unbearable, a radiant light appeared on the horizon, a brightness that filled the air with warmth and reassurance. He recognized this light instantly—it was his own Second Coming, a beacon of hope that signified the final fulfillment of his mission on earth. The sight of it brought a quiet peace, a reminder that all he was enduring would one day be complete, and humanity's redemption would be fully realized. Jesus' heart was now filled with the sins that were, are, and will come to be. His heart, though fully human, was sustained by a love so boundless that it could contain what no other could. He took a deep, steadying breath, wiping the blood-streaked sweat from his brow, and whispered a prayer of gratitude to the Father. The angel of the Lord lovingly assisted Jesus onto his feet. The angel embraced Jesus like a child, hugging their father, clinging to him with a mixture of awe, need, and love that strengthened him. The angel brought him peace, and then, with his bright eyes filling with tears, the angel left Jesus alone in the garden.

In the distance, Jesus glimpsed the faint glow of torches moving steadily toward him, flickering lights in the darkness that marked the approach of those who would soon lead him to his fate. He knew they were coming for him, the final step of his earthly mission now beginning to unfold. The hour was upon him, and so he went to wake the others.

Then he returned to his disciples and said to them, "Are you still sleeping and taking your rest? Behold, the hour is at hand when the Son of Man is to be handed over to sinners. Get up, let us go. Look, my betrayer is at hand."

—Matthew 26:45–46

"In Gethsemane the holiest of all petitioners prayed three times that a certain cup might pass from Him. It did not."

—C. S. Lewis

"Each betrayal begins with trust."

—Martin Luther

CHAPTER 2

The Pillar

───●─●───

A s Peter and the other disciples rose to their feet, a wave of shame washed over them. They had fallen asleep while Jesus prayed in agony, leaving him alone in his darkest hour. They heard a small crowd nearby heading in their direction. They were not sure who was coming or why, but they noticed Judas was among the group holding torches. Leading the group, they recognized Judas, clutching a torch as he walked among an ominous-looking mob, men armed with clubs and swords, their expressions hard and unyielding. The flickering torchlight cast shadows across their faces, revealing some as temple guards, men whose intent was unmistakably sinister.

Jesus had seen the torchlight flickering in the distance, and he knew exactly who was coming and why. He stood resolute as the others fell into silence, watching Judas approach. He and the others watched as Judas approached. The steps Judas took were uncertain. Judas's steps were hesitant, as though he might abandon his dark purpose and return to the Twelve, but his resolve hardened with each step. He reached Jesus, eyes clouded with turmoil, and leaned forward, pressing a kiss to his cheek, a gesture of betrayal cloaked in the reverence of the word he whispered: "Rabbi."

Jesus answered him, "Friend, do what you have come for."

—Matthew 26:50

Judas motioned to the guards and stepped aside, making way for them to come and arrest Jesus. The guards rushed forward, grabbed him, and quickly bound his hands. Rough hands gripped the rope around him, jerking it as they forced him forward. Yet, even in this moment, Jesus turned back toward Judas, his soft brown eyes full of a love that reached beyond the betrayal. For a lingering moment, he held Judas's gaze, offering forgiveness that Judas could neither comprehend nor bear until the encroaching darkness finally came between them.

Judas knew at that moment that Jesus was forgiving him. Judas recognized Jesus' expression. Over the last few years, he had seen it many times. It was the same look he had seen countless times—when Jesus had healed the sick, restored the lost, forgiven the sinner. As the shadows closed around Jesus, Judas found he could not look away. Those eyes, filled with boundless mercy, seemed to speak to him: "My son, I have already forgiven you this night." What he didn't know was that Jesus had already accepted this betrayal in the solitude of the garden, surrendering his heart to the Father's will for the sake of humanity.

He knew that man's sins must be forgiven to glorify God the Father and for them to have a chance at salvation. Out of love for all people everywhere, Jesus accepted the Father's will, no matter the cost.

As Jesus' form faded into the shadows, so too did Judas's last semblance of hope. He reached instinctively for the pouch at his side, feeling the cold press of the thirty silver coins—the hollow price of his betrayal. Their weight now bore down on him like a millstone, each coin a reminder of what he had forfeited. The coins became an anchor, and their weight became unbearable. At that moment, there in darkness, Judas became aware that he was cold and alone. He no longer lived in the light of Christ. The light of Christ, which he had once walked in, was now beyond his reach, leaving him shrouded in the shadows of his own making.

For the first time, Judas understood the depth and beauty of Jesus' love—a love that reached beyond forgiveness, a love that embraced even betrayal. Yet now, as he stood cloaked in the darkness of his own making, it felt as though an impenetrable curtain had fallen between them. Now, as Judas tried to picture Jesus in his mind, he could not. All he could see was the chief priest giving him the ransom money. He saw only greed and sins. Nothing else would come to him. He realized that his calculated arrest of Jesus was really his own demise. His act of betrayal had not secured anything or worth; instead, it had stripped him of all hope.

Judas wildly ran into the darkness with tears in his eyes as he panicked, frantically seeking a way to make things right. The darkness around him pressed in, cold and unyielding; he yearned to escape it, to return to the light he had once known—the light of Christ. Driven by the desperation that he might somehow make amends, he clutched the silver coins and ran toward the temple elders, intent on returning the money, as though doing so might buy back both Jesus' life and his own.

Jesus, meanwhile, was being led away to the temple by the guards. His disciples followed at a distance, their hearts heavy with worry and confusion, keeping just close enough to see him but far enough to remain unnoticed. Fear clouded their understanding, and they struggled to grasp the gravity of what was unfolding. Jesus' tether was pulled on by one of the guards like he was an animal heading for slaughter. The guards wasted no time. They wanted to get Jesus to the temple as soon as possible, so they kept a fast and steady pace. The guard who led Jesus would yank on the tether whenever he thought Jesus was not walking fast enough. He also had a habit of doing this every time they changed direction. With each jerk of the tether, a thought rose in Jesus' mind: If they treat the innocent like this, what mercy could they ever show to the guilty?

They finally reached the temple steps, and Jesus glanced over his shoulder. His eyes met Peter's as he saw a few of the apostles approaching the temple area. Peter's face was etched with worry, his eyes filled with a doubt that Jesus had not seen in him for some time. In that moment, Jesus sensed the depth of Peter's inner struggle, understanding that his beloved disciple's faith, already fragile, was about to face its most severe trial. He felt a pang of sorrow for Peter, knowing that the hours to come would test him in ways he could scarcely imagine.

Peter looked at Jesus and stopped walking. He stood there frozen in his spot, watching as the guards led Jesus into the temple. Rooted to the spot, he watched helplessly as the guards led Jesus away, guiding him up the temple steps and into the shadowed interior. Inside, Jesus was brought to the center of a grand room, where a gathering of scribes and elders awaited, their expressions steeled with judgment. The air was thick with tension, and Peter felt a heaviness settle over him as he remained outside, watching the teacher he loved be delivered into the hands of those who sought his end.

It was clear this was an orchestrated scheme, a trap carefully laid under the cover of night—the hour when shadows concealed truth and emboldened those who acted in malice. Jesus knew the light of truth would not shine in this place. He noticed that the entire council had not assembled. Jesus had friends among the Jewish leaders, but many of them were absent. Many of those who might have spoken for him were conspicuously absent, leaving him surrounded by those determined to see him fall. In the heart of darkness, the Prince of Light awaited his fate, a solitary figure shining in defiance of the shadows.

Jesus was aware the chief priest and the members of the Sanhedrin were attempting to find some reason to put him to death, but none could be found. Many came forward to bear false witness against him, but there was no one who could verify these witnesses. One by one, false witnesses stepped forward, their claims hollow and conflicting, each attempt to condemn him unraveling under scrutiny. Among those gathered were a few who held reverence for him—scribes and priests who, though outnumbered, believed in his righteousness and even dared to hope he was the Son of God. They spoke out, countering each falsehood with truth, their words erasing the accusations like shadows chased away by light. With each defense, the lies dissolved. Tempers elevated, and the conversation became a shouting match. The room erupted with aggression, both sides refusing to back down from their arguments.

This conflict led to confusion and angered the chief priest. Jesus tried not to smile when this took place. He knew that an expression of happiness would only enrage the priest more. What made him smile, however, was knowing his Father was at work. He knew he was going to be sentenced to death, but that it would be because of the truth, not a lie. Silently, he thanked the Father for the few voices speaking in his defense, confident that his life would stand as a testament of love and sacrifice—a legacy that would echo in the hearts of the faithful long after this night had ended.

The room became more hostile and angrier as time passed. People shouted at each other. Allies turned into adversaries as lifelong bonds were forgotten in the heat of the moment, their shouts clashing like swords drawn in battle. The scribes and priests were divided among themselves. The few who argued on Jesus' behalf were outnumbered, but they would not concede to the unjust sentencing of one they considered an innocent man. The argument raged on until a voice, out of the deafening mayhem, echoed off the stone walls. It said: *"This man said, 'I can destroy the temple of God and within three days rebuild it'"* (Matthew 26:61).

In that moment, everyone fell silent. Not another word was spoken, and the energy in the room stayed suspended in the air. It was a true pause in time. It felt as though even the winds outside ceased their whispering, the sea held its breath, and all of creation stood still, caught in the profound stillness that followed the accusation. The universe seemed frozen, waiting in solemn anticipation of what would come next.

This pause was eventually broken by another witness who came forward and verified the testimony. Everyone in the room knew these words had been spoken by Jesus, yet no one, not even any of his followers, believed it could be done.

Jesus looked around the room and studied the faces of the men before him. In the eyes of those who supported him, he saw desperation mingled with quiet despair. They strained to find words that might defend him, yet the fear of sounding foolish held their tongues. He could tell they were trying with all their might to think of something to say in his defense without sounding like fools. Jesus knew these were righteous men, and he was grateful for them. They were not skilled in the art of deceit, and they did not possess poisonous tongues. They would not be able to twist Jesus' words to come to his aid, nor did he want them to do so. Forever, they would be remembered for their valiant effort to defend Jesus.

He looked into the eyes of these men and collected this moment in his mind. He would make sure that later, in heaven, the Father would glorify these men who had come to his defense. Jesus was humbled by their compassion and would remember them always.

Jesus turned his gaze to the rest of the assembly. He could see how their demeanor had immediately changed. Furrowed brows lifted, and eyes that had once glared with intensity now gleamed with cunning satisfaction. The dark lines caused by so many years in the desert sun were deepening by the smiles emerging from their wicked thoughts. These were men who thrived on moments of advantage, and they grasped the implications of the testimony that had just been spoken. They knew its weight and sensed the opportunity it offered to fulfill their intentions.

Caiaphas, the high priest, approached Jesus. "So, tell us, Jesus of Galilee, you claim to be able to destroy this Temple and rebuild it in three days? How can you accomplish such a feat, a feat no other man can do?"

Jesus looked deeply through Caiaphas' eyes and into his soul. He saw a man entirely uninterested in the truth; in fact, Caiaphas was afraid of it. What he saw was not a seeker of truth, but a man gripped by fear—fear of the upheaval that truth would bring, fear of losing the fragile grip on power and prestige that defined him. Jesus knew this man, and those who supported him would never accept the truth.

Jesus prayed silently to the Father. Dear heavenly Father, give your wisdom in my words. But as Jesus waited, nothing came to him to say. He understood that in this chamber, clouded by human pride and corrupted by ambition, the truth had become something beyond defense. How far had this generation strayed to shut their hearts so completely to the light and majesty of the Father? Jesus wondered. This thought solidified his conviction that now was the time for him to be glorified. Now more than ever, humanity needed a savior.

Jesus stood silently, staring at Caiaphas. The priest prodded Jesus to answer the question, but Jesus refused to say anything. Caiaphas, growing tired of Jesus' refusal to answer, barked out, "I order you, under oath before the living God, to tell us: Are you the Messiah, the Son of God?" The words rang out, echoing in the chamber, as all eyes turned to Jesus, awaiting his response with breathless anticipation.

Jesus felt the calm presence of the Father within, and he knew now was the time. There was no sense in delaying the predetermined outcome of this hearing.

Jesus said to him in reply, "You have said so. But I tell you: From now on you will see 'the Son of Man seated at the right hand of the Power' and 'coming on the clouds of heaven.'"

—Matthew 26:64

With rage forming on Caiaphas's face, the priest reached up, grabbed his own robes, and tore them, screaming, *"He has blasphemed! What further need have we of witnesses? You have now heard the blasphemy; what is your opinion?' They said in reply, 'He deserves to die!'"* (Matthew 26:65-66).

At that moment, the anger in the room shifted to violence. Caiaphas was the first to swing at Jesus, hitting his face with the back of his hand. The sharp sting jolted through Jesus, and the taste of blood filled his mouth, but he steadied himself, standing tall as Caiaphas stepped closer, spitting into his face with disdain. Jesus instinctively raised his bound hands to wipe his cheek, but another swift blow came before he could move, causing blood to flow freely from his lips. The air thickened with animosity, each strike a testament to the anger these men felt that was a result of their ignorance.

The violence escalated quickly. It was as though each priest and scribe wanted a turn to strike and spit at the Son of Man. Blow after blow rained down upon him, each one carrying the weight of their scorn. Unable to shield himself, Jesus staggered under the onslaught, finally collapsing to the ground, and then struggled to regain a standing position. With his hands bound and the angry crowd pressing in on him, he was helpless to do anything but endure the beating.

The assault continued, relentless and merciless. Blow after blow fell upon him, each strike leaving a fresh mark, bruises blossoming across his skin like shadows of their disdain. One of his eyes had swollen shut, his nose was bleeding, and the taste of blood lingered, sharp and bitter. Pain coursed through every part of his body, a symphony of bruises and lacerations that painted a tapestry of suffering from head to toe. Finally, Caiaphas called for an end to the violence and ordered Jesus to be taken by the guards to be held until they could take him to Pontius Pilate to be sentenced to death. As Jesus was led from the chamber, the temple was quickly emptied, shadows receding with the first hints of dawn. Caiaphas was careful; he wanted no risk of the morning light drawing out any who might come to defend Jesus. It was easier, far easier, to keep this deed cloaked in darkness, away from prying eyes and the celebration that would soon fill the streets.

When the morning sun broke through the darkness of the night, Jesus was taken before Pontius Pilate. Pilate, while pondering Jesus' arrest, questioned the Sanhedrin, asking what Jesus had been charged with. "Blasphemy," they declared, the word falling heavy in the air. But Pilate, unshaken, dismissed them with a wave, uninterested in the charge that bore no weight in Roman law. "This is a matter of your own," he told them, "A question of your beliefs and customs. Take him to Herod, your own leader, and let him decide." With that, Jesus was once more led away, the judgment deferred yet again.

Much to their displeasure, the chief priest ordered the guards to take Jesus to Herod. When word reached Herod, he received it with unmistakable delight, his eyes lighting up with the thrill of anticipation. He had wanted to meet Jesus, having heard of the many signs and wonders that were associated with Jesus' name. Herod was hopeful that Jesus would perform some miracles while in his presence.

When Jesus was brought into Herod's chambers and placed before him, Herod approached Jesus slowly, trying to decide what to think. His gaze swept over this man over this man who claimed to be the King of the Jews, the one whose kingdom was said to be eternal. But to Herod's eyes, there was no majesty, no grandeur—only a man in ruin. Jesus stood bloodied and disheveled, his face swollen, his hair matted with blood and dust, his clothing torn and stained from repeated assaults that had left him collapsed on the ground. His hands were filthy from clutching the earth in moments of torment, his dignity intact even as his body bore the marks of a thorough beating.

Herod viewed Jesus as a beggar, not a king. He did not have the appearance of a person who commanded respect. When Herod questioned Jesus about his status, Jesus did not respond. Herod then requested Jesus perform a miracle in his presence, but Jesus knew this was nothing more than Herod trying to find amusement in what he anticipated to be grand parlor tricks. Jesus did not respond again.

Herod, looking into Jesus' eyes, found no threat to his throne. In fact, he found nothing at all. Jesus appeared to be devoid of emotion. Herod found no fear, no ambition, not even anger. There was a depth in Jesus that Herod could not understand, a silence filled with purpose that left him unnerved. The salvation Jesus offered held no appeal to him; his heart was tied to the pleasures of the flesh, to the allure of power and indulgence that had become his world.

Herod, finding no fault, threat, or amusement in Jesus, dismissed both him and the Sanhedrin, even though they were still insisting that Jesus was a criminal.

The Jews, refusing to be deterred, continued to look for a way to put Jesus to death. They were desperate to ensure he not be elevated in status by escaping their judgment. Failure was not an option—they saw in him a spark that, left unchecked, could ignite a movement beyond their control. And so, once again, Jesus was led back to Pilate, his fate now resting in the hands of a man torn between justice and the relentless demands of the crowd.

Pilate inquired, *"You brought this man to me and accused him of inciting the people to revolt. I have conducted my investigation in your presence and have not found this man guilty of the charges that you have brought against him, nor did Herod, for he sent him back to us. So no capital crime has been committed by him. Therefore I shall have him flogged and then release him"* (Luke 23:13–17).

At this announcement, the crowd erupted, immediately becoming angry and wild. The devil would not be denied his day to see the Son of Man suffer. He knew of men's wicked thoughts, and he used them to his advantage. From somewhere in the ravenous crowd, a voice screamed out, "Release Barabbas!" Barabbas was a criminal of the vilest sort, a son of Satan. This call pleased the devil, for Barabbas was one of his own, and the idea of his freedom fanned the flames of darkness within the crowd. They knew it was customary to release a prisoner during the Passover feast. They did not want Jesus released, so they encouraged the crowd by continuing to yell out, "Release Barabbas! Release Barabbas!" Soon, the entire crowd cried out in unison to release the criminal Barabbas.

Pilate was uneasy about this request. He did not want the Jews to revolt and get out of hand, for he knew it would be considered his fault for not controlling the situation since it was in his own court that the violence was beginning. Neither did he feel comfortable condemning a man he considered innocent nor releasing a violent criminal back into the general population.

Pilate said to them, "Then what shall I do with Jesus called Messiah?" They all said, "Let him be crucified!" But he said, "Why? What evil has he done?" They only shouted out louder, "Let him be crucified!" When Pilate saw that he was not succeeding at all, but a riot was breaking out instead, he took water and washed his hands in the sight of the crowd, saying, "I am innocent of this man's blood. Look to it yourselves." And the whole people said in reply, "His blood be upon us and upon our children."

—Matthew 27:22–25

The Roman guards seized Jesus, leading him away from the crowd's relentless cries and into the shadows of the inner courtyard. In silence, he braced himself, already feeling the sting of the lash in his mind, each imagined blow a prelude to what he knew lay ahead. They pushed him down a narrow stone corridor, its walls cold and close, the light barely penetrating the dark passage. The guard behind him prodded him forward with a staff, pressing it firmly into his lower back, forcing each step. The path was tight, confining, as though the walls themselves bore witness to the suffering endured within them.

The corridor eventually opened into a stark, expansive courtyard—a barren place devoid of even the smallest sign of life. No greenery softened the cold stone; no tree offered shelter or shade. Every inch of the courtyard was made of hard, unyielding rock. The rock had been well-hewn and expertly placed, but the lifelessness of this courtyard seemed to echo in desolation as if the very stones mourned in silent solidarity with the cruelty they had witnessed.

As Jesus entered the courtyard, a crowd had already begun to gather, drawn by rumors that spread like wildfire. Men and women jostled for position, eager to secure a vantage point from which to witness the brutal spectacle about to unfold. The balconies above filled quickly, lined with onlookers whose eyes gleamed with a morbid anticipation. The faithless and the curious alike had come, drawn not by reverence but by a fascination with the suffering of another—a madman, they thought, whose punishment would be their morning's entertainment. Jesus knew the hearts of these men. No matter how many times they heard or experienced the truth, it eluded them because they were men of the flesh.

There were those who came with little faith. They believed in God but were skeptical of Jesus. They came to see if he would save himself from punishment. If he was truly the Son of God, they thought, he would not allow this to happen, but rather, he would do something spectacular to stop it. They would then get to witness his power and glory and praise the new Messiah, but they would need to see a miracle for themselves to believe.

There were also those of weak faith. These men believed Jesus was a holy man of God, but they were prone to live in the flesh and not the Spirit. They did, after all, love Jesus and all that he stood for. They wanted to live in his image, but they lacked the necessary courage. They could not find the strength within themselves to give up their possessions or their social status. Their hearts ached with reverence, but courage eluded them, the fear of surrendering fully to God too great a cost. They came that morning not in certainty but in hope, praying that someone might intervene, that a hand would stay the whip and spare him the torment he was about to endure.

And then there were those of unwavering, profound faith—the devoted ones who loved him beyond measure and had come that day with a single purpose: to pray. Jesus felt the weight of their love as they gathered, their hearts breaking at the sight of their beloved teacher bound and beaten, yet their spirits resolute. They whispered their prayers, their voices rising as quiet pleas to the heavens, each word carried on the wings of sorrow and devotion. Tears streamed down their faces, mingling with their words, transforming each prayer into an offering of love, reaching the Father in earnest hope for mercy. Jesus was humiliated as he was stripped publicly and then forced to his knees. His hands were bound and secured slightly above his head to a pillar. He watched as the guards discussed the appropriate instrument with which to inflict the pain, as well as who would be the one to inflict it.

Jesus' mind raced with anticipation, and he started to breathe heavily. He looked around and saw a small group of his disciples gathered in one spot. They had faces that were awash in fear and sadness. For a brief moment, his thoughts drifted to the Parable of the Sower, wondering if they now understood what he had tried to teach them that day, how the seeds of faith would find their soil in times of trial. Lost in memory, he almost felt the warmth of that teaching moment again, but the present reality pulled him back to the cold stone beneath his knees.

"A sower went out to sow. And as he sowed, some seed fell on the path, and birds came and ate it up. Some fell on rocky ground, where it had little soil. It sprang up at once because the soil was not deep, as when the sun rose it was scorched, and it withered for lack of roots. Some seed fell among thorns, and the thorns grew up and choked it. But some seed fell on rich soil, and produced fruit, a hundred or sixty or thirtyfold. Whoever has ears ought to hear."

—Matthew 13:3–9

Today, Jesus saw the same frightened and confused looks in their eyes that he had seen on that day. However, today, it seemed amplified. As he met their gazes, a warmth flooded his heart, a gentle reassurance that, though they did not yet fully understand, they would someday grasp the depth of all he had taught them. It comforted him to know they were near, their presence a quiet testament to their love and faith. In that moment, he lifted his heart in silent prayer for them, asking the Father to strengthen them, to grant them peace, and to open their hearts to the understanding that would one day sustain them.

Jesus opened his eyes and looked around again. He saw that the balconies were at their maximum capacity and that the crowd on the ground level had increased greatly. There was no more room to stand and see, so people were constantly repositioning themselves as they tried to gain a better vantage point. The Roman guards were forced to push the crowd back so they would not overcome the area where Jesus was tied.

As the people in the crowd pushed for room to stand, they swayed like penned sheep. Jesus noticed a small gap in the crowd under one of the arched balconies. At first, he did not see who was there, but it felt cold. The devil himself had come to witness the beating of the Son of Man. When the devil knew Jesus sensed him, he parted the crowd so they could make eye contact. That day, three years before—when the devil had offered Jesus the world and had been rejected—was still fresh in his mind. The devil's gaze held a dark invitation as though ready to make his twisted offer once more. But Jesus would not allow it; he knew the devil's true intent went far beyond tempting him personally. This time, the devil desired not to claim Jesus himself but the weight he bore within his heart—the sins of all humanity. But Jesus stood resolute, unyielding, his spirit fortified by a love stronger than any darkness. The sacrifice he prepared to make was not one he would surrender, no matter how the devil sought to corrupt it.

The devil, after trying many times to communicate with Jesus, realized he did not possess the power to do so. This enraged the devil, and his spirit left the small opening. In an instant, the small void in the crowd filled in, yet the devil's presence remained, now focused elsewhere. Without hesitation, he turned his sights to the guards, seeking a vessel for his malevolence. He entered the prison guard who had been appointed to oversee the flogging, darkening the man's heart, and from the depths of hell summoned another spirit to inhabit the one who would wield the whip. Suddenly, the guards' discussion ceased. Their eyes hardened, and without a word, they prepared to carry out the brutality as if compelled by an unseen hand.

The possessed guard picked up a whip and headed for Jesus. Without warning, he raised the whip high and brought it down with full, merciless force. The impact tore through Jesus' body, a searing pain radiating from his back and gripping his entire being. He arched his back and was forced up on his toes by the sting. His body desperately tried to distance itself from the pain but could not. His eyes clenched shut, filling with tears as the brutal lash burned its way into his flesh, his chest pressing hard against the steadfast pillar that held him. The pillar against which he leaned was rough, worn by countless torments, its surface tainted with the lingering scent of sweat, blood, and suffering. The stains on its weathered wood told silent stories of the countless souls who had endured agony here before him, and in that instant, Jesus felt a profound compassion well within him—for all who had borne such pain. But his moment of empathy was shattered as the whip struck again, tearing through his flesh like fire. Each lash felt as though it were made not of leather but of flame itself, searing through him with merciless intensity, his body recoiling under the onslaught. As it came across his back, the blow initially forced his body to arch and his eyes to close and water. However, the burn that was the after effect caused his hands to shake and his knees to feel weak.

Again, the whip came forcefully down, snapping at the skin of his back, this time from the opposite direction. The possessed guard had moved to make sure that this time, the whip left a new mark as it crossed the open wounds he had already made. It was obvious that the guard was trying to inflict as much pain as possible.

The relentless burn of the whip tore through him, each stroke unsettling his balance as the pain spread in waves. His stomach twisted in anguish, churning with such intensity that he fought the urge to collapse under the weight of it. Only the bindings around his wrists kept him upright, his hands fastened high above his head to the pillar. Had he not been bound, he knew he would have crumpled to the ground, the agony too great for any mortal frame to bear on its own.

At this point, blood was running freely down Jesus' back. His abuser was skilled in the art of torture and talented enough to draw vast amounts of blood with his instrument. Jesus felt weak. He found himself leaning against the pillar for support. The foul and rotten odor of the blood and flesh stained on the pillar filled his nose and mind. He embraced the pillar as if it were a brother. No matter how foul the pillar may have been, it was the only thing helping Jesus at that moment. He embraced it because he knew he was leaving blood and sweat on it like those before him had, and the next person tied to this post would smell his fouled blood.

His heart thundered within his chest, each beat echoing the brutal rhythm of the whip as it tore into his back. The guard, now pausing between strikes, seemed to survey his wounds, searching for unmarked skin where fresh lashes could be inflicted. Jesus' back was a canvas of agony, raw and bleeding, a testament to the savagery he was enduring. With each successive blow, his body trembled uncontrollably, his hands bound above him, supporting more and more of his weight as his legs grew weak beneath him. The bindings cut deeper into his wrists as he leaned heavily into them, the torture exacting a toll that seemed endless.

With each passing lash, Jesus felt his strength slipping, his body growing more fragile with the relentless assault. The devil, lurking and watchful, had anticipated this very moment—the moment when exhaustion would cloud Jesus' senses, where pain might erode his defenses. Now, as Jesus fought to hold onto consciousness, the devil seized his chance, slipping into the periphery of his thoughts.

Jesus heard the devil's voice in his head. Son of Man, let go of what is mine, and I will end your pain. Jesus did not answer. The devil, who had once tempted Jesus and tried to get him to bow before him, was no longer interested in gaining Jesus' allegiance. He was after what Jesus guarded in his heart, and he knew he could not get there; Jesus would have to give them up freely. To the devil, the sins of humankind were his prize, the emblem of his influence, his twisted mark upon creation. They were his dominion, his pride—proof of his power to sway hearts away from the light. In his view, each sin was a victory, each lost soul a tribute to his supremacy as the great tempter. And now, seeing Jesus bear these sins with unwavering resolve, the devil felt his grip slipping. He knew that should forgiveness prevail, he would lose the souls he'd claimed as his own, and the thought filled him with furious envy. He could not bear to see the Son of Man glorified, not while the weight of mankind's sins rested upon him.

Again, he approached Jesus. Your human heart was not made to endure such suffering. Eventually, you will fail. The voice grew darker, more threatening, laced with bitter malice. "Deny me, and I will show you a pain beyond this—a depth of agony that no mortal heart can bear." Yet Jesus remained silent, unshaken, his strength rooted in a purpose beyond the devil's grasp. His resolve was a light no darkness could dim.

With this, the whip crashed down across the back of his legs. It was as though a new and tender spot had been found. Jesus' back was becoming numb from the whipping, but his legs were untouched. This concerned him because he was counting on them for support when this was over. His breath was very deep, and he could feel his heart begin to beat harder and faster as his tormentor continued to find fresh flesh to cut with the whip. Jesus' body burned intensely. The burning spread through him, fierce and consuming, until it felt as if his very blood pulsed with flames. Weakness seeped into his limbs, but still, he endured, holding fast to the resolve within.

At Jesus' refusal to yield, the devil's voice rang out in his mind. If you do not release what is mine, I will beat you until every drop of your blood is spilled here and the sins of the world drain out of your heart as the blood pours out onto the ground. The sins of man are mine! It was your God who put me here. The earth and these people are my domain. Your God has his heaven, his angels, his minions, but these people are mine. They are filled with my desires. They are filled with vanity, jealousy, fear, pride, greed, and hate. These are my virtues, not yours. What do you want with them!? They are not worthy of your pain or sacrifice. They are warriors for my cause, not yours or your God's. Release what you stole from me!

With a voice trembling yet resolute, Jesus spoke, defying the darkness that surrounded him. "They are my children," he answered, his words carrying the weight of boundless love. "You know the Father's love for his children, and you know what kind of Father he is. His love is my love, and as he loves them, so do I. Their sins are no longer yours to claim—they are mine to bear. It is the love of the Father that strengthens me, a love that endures beyond any darkness." With unwavering finality, he declared, "Away with you, Satan. You have no place here."

Once the devil had been cast off, he became enraged. The head guard, whom the devil had possessed, stood and, with fury, yelled out to the guard doing the beating, "I want his blood to run like a river in the streets. Beat him!"

The guard wielding the whip was weary, his body taxed by the brutality he had already unleashed, his breath labored. His possessor, however, obeyed the devil's command. And with renewed energy and as much hatred as possible, he began to whip Jesus as violently as humanly possible. Gone was any calculated cruelty—now he struck blindly, violently, unleashing a torrent of blows meant to break body and spirit alike.

Amid the onslaught, Jesus hardly registered the crowd, their voices a distant clamor at the edge of his awareness. Men's shouts mingled with women's cries, their reactions woven with both horror and bitter delight. He also heard some of the people cheering with every blow of the whip. They would laugh as Jesus cried out in pain from the burn of each blow.

In a fleeting moment of stillness, Jesus opened his eyes, blurred with tears, and his gaze found her—his mother. Her face was resolute, her expression a mask of strength, yet her eyes betrayed the depth of her sorrow, glistening with tears she refused to shed. She stood steadfast, a pillar of quiet strength amid the crowd, holding herself together for her beloved Son. Though her heart ached with a pain beyond words, she would not let herself break—not now, not when he needed her presence more than anything. Powerless to ease his suffering, she stood rooted in her love, a silent vow of support. In that unspoken exchange, he knew she was with him, her silent strength a balm to his breaking heart. As his gaze lingered on his mother, a silent plea rose within him: Please, Father, if it is Your will, let this end—not for my sake, but for hers.

The guard was becoming unsteady from fatigue. His own motions were setting him off balance with every blow, but he continued to beat Jesus relentlessly just the same. Jesus held the pillar, clinging to it with all his strength, praying the torture would soon end.

The devil, enraged with anger at Jesus' determination to hold the sins of man in his heart, became discouraged and fled the head guard. Freed from the devil's influence, the guard stood in the courtyard, dazed and unaware of the darkness that had clouded his actions. Slowly, he turned to see Jesus' battered form, his face paling as realization dawned. A look of horror crept over him as he took in the sight before him—the bloodied, broken man lying helplessly on the stone floor. Shock mingled with disbelief, for he could scarcely reconcile the brutality he had inflicted with his own hands.

Jesus no longer had the strength to hold himself upright. His body hung limp, suspended by his bound wrists, his full weight straining his shoulders to the breaking point. Pain surged through his arms, the pressure threatening to tear his joints apart as he swayed against the pillar. Blood trickled steadily from his wounds, forming a dark, growing pool surrounding his limp body, a silent testament to the suffering he bore. The head guard was unsure of what was happening, but he knew it had to stop summoning what authority he had left, he called out, "Enough! This man has suffered enough!"

His voice rang out in the courtyard, cutting through the clamor as if to restore a sliver of humanity to the brutal scene. At his command, the dark influence over the other guard lifted, leaving him as shaken and uncertain as his superior. The guard who had beaten Jesus was exhausted and covered in blood. He looked down at his own body and dropped the whip from his hand in shock. He was dismayed and confused. He had carried out countless punishments, accustomed to the brutality of his role, but this— this was different. The sight of Jesus' ravaged body unsettled him deeply, and he struggled to understand how he had been capable of inflicting such suffering.

The head guard ordered the other guards to remove Jesus from the pillar and disperse the crowd. There were those who wanted the beating to continue, and they yelled and screamed for more. The head guard, fearing the crowd would get out of hand, quickly ordered the other guards to drive everyone away. Two other guards then picked Jesus' limp body up to release him from the pillar. At first, he could not stand. The guards had to hold him up while his chains were removed. The shackles used to bind his hands left deep marks on his wrist from his weight. Freed from the shackles, a fleeting sense of relief passed through him, but his body remained engulfed in pain, each step an agony of its own.

Every cell of his body was in pain. As the guards tried to escort him from the courtyard, it was clear he could not walk on his own yet, so they forcefully carried him along. Jesus' body trembled uncontrollably, every nerve frayed and raw from the relentless brutality. His skin, torn open in countless places, bore the marks of deep suffering, his wounds weeping blood and fluid that streaked his body. As he walked away from the location of his abuse, being half-carried by several guards, He began to take long, deep breaths. He tried to calm his mind and stop the violent shaking.

The guards led him out of the courtyard and back through the stone passageway that had brought him to this torturous event. They eventually reached a small, dimly lit room, where they returned his torn, blood-stained garments. As he sank down onto the hard floor, relief washed over him—not for the pain itself, but for its end, however brief. With a heart full of gratitude, he offered silent thanks to the Father, grateful for the strength that had carried him through the trial, sustaining him in the face of unthinkable suffering.

Back in the courtyard, the guard who had delivered the whipping was still standing in the same spot. The courtyard had been emptied of the crowd. He stood alone, staring at the bloodstained pillar. The ground around him was also covered in blood. How had he inflicted such suffering without fully grasping it? He felt as if he'd been overtaken by something dark and unfamiliar, an influence he could neither understand nor control. He knew he had administered the beating. He was covered in blood, and he remembered dropping the whip. But what had happened to him? He did not know what had caused him to act so violently. The image of Jesus' torn skin was etched in his mind. Did I really do all of that? He wondered. Have I become such an animal that I no longer am aware of my actions? The man was tormented by the vision before him. A wooden pillar, which was normally a deep brown color from age and weather, was now red with blood. Jesus' face was clear in his mind, and the guard asked himself, what did this man do to deserve this? He had been an instrument of torture many times before, but he had always remembered his actions. This time, it was as if the images of him whipping Jesus seemed obscured and distant. He had flogged many criminals and been dispassionate about it. But in that moment, he knew that what had happened that day was different in some way. He was different in some ways. He did not know how or why, but things had changed for him forever.

As he stood there staring at the pillar, he thought about his life. All that he had taken for granted in his life no longer made sense. Lost in his thoughts, he glanced down at the whip lying at his feet, then back at the pillar. The realization dawned upon him with unexpected force: he could no longer be the instrument of such suffering. The desire to inflict pain had drained from him entirely, replaced by a yearning for something unknown—a path that healed rather than harmed. With one last look at the pillar, he turned and walked away, knowing deep within that he could never return to this life.

With each step he took from the courtyard, he felt the weight of his old life slipping away. What he had known, what he had been, faded with every footfall as if the very ground were absorbing the remnants of who he once was. That day marked the beginning of a search for something deeper, a life rooted not in obedience to orders but in the pursuit of redemption and purpose.

CHAPTER 3

A Crown of Thorns

———— •◆• ————

As Jesus sat in the room where he was placed, he closed his eyes to rest. He had not slept the previous night, and he was tired from the lack of sleep and the torture he'd endured. He was very aware of his wounds. Every inch of his being was painfully aware of his wounds. He leaned back, hoping to ease his fatigue, but the pain radiating from his torn flesh flared unbearably, forbidding even the slightest comfort. The room, a stark and barren cell, was meant only to contain, not to console; all it offered was a cold stone bench. He gave up trying to sit on the bench and recline, choosing instead to lie flat on his chest. As he slowly and painfully adjusted his position, he felt the pain of his clothes brushing across his wounded skin. The blood was drying, causing his tunic to stick. As he moved, it tore away from his skin, bringing yet more pain for him to suffer through. Jesus struggled to get into a position that could even come close to be considered comfortable. After several moments, he finally settled on a position that caused less discomfort than the rest. The cool stone beneath him pressed against his fevered skin, a small, soothing salve to his burning wounds. His back radiated such intense heat from the searing pain that he imagined his very sweat rising as steam, escaping from the agony that refused to leave him. It felt good to be at rest. As Jesus sat there alone with his thoughts, his childhood raced through his mind. Warm thoughts of his mother and father filled his head. He remembered the quiet conversations his mother had had with him about the importance of being faithful to God in heaven. He remembered her gentle urging to care for the poor, to love others without reserve, as if each person were a cherished soul. He adored hearing his mother speak about his heavenly Father. Her eyes were soft, and her voice was calm and always filled with love. Listening to his mother speak was like listening to a gentle breeze. It was never harsh or cold; it was always warm and inviting. Her sincere love for God gave her voice the tone of an angel and the warmth of the sun on a summer morning. The genuine love she had for everyone gave her words meaning and purpose. Jesus was glad to have his mother so close, at least in his thoughts. It brought him much comfort, and he smiled as a picture of her face formed in his mind. Her beauty and grace were unmatched here on earth. He loved her and felt loved by her. In his heart, he wished more people would love him and the Father as much as his mother did. If that were the case, maybe he wouldn't have to suffer through all of this. If people would just fill their hearts with love, the world would be a much different place.

The warm vision of love and comfort slowly dissolved, overtaken by the stark weight of mankind's sins. When will they understand? he wondered. Is it truly so hard to choose the path of obedience, to walk toward God's light rather than cling to fear and darkness? This thought had run through Jesus' mind more often than he cared to admit in the past few years. While he proclaimed the Good News, he met so many people who could not believe. "How foolish is this generation?" he said aloud.

Jesus shook his head in frustration, and the moment of peace was immediately replaced by pain. He shifted slightly, and his tunic, bonded to his wounds by dried blood, tore painfully from his skin. The back of the fabric clung to him like a second, tortured layer of flesh, reopening cuts that had barely begun to scab over. He froze, attempting to relieve himself of the pain, but he was caught out of position. His head was elevated, and his back was arched. Given his weakened state, it would only be a matter of minutes before his neck fatigued. Jesus tried to lower his head slowly, but this caused a systematic tearing away of the cloth that had fused itself to his wounds, exposing his open scars to new sections of the tunic. There was no use in avoiding the inevitable. He quickly lowered his head and repositioned himself for comfort. This caused much of the cloth that was stuck to his wounds to tear away from his back all at once. He gritted his teeth and closed his eyes tightly from the pain, but Jesus was happy to be settled. He could feel many wounds tear open on his back and blood running down his sides. He knew he would have to go through it all again the next time he had to move, but for now, he was settled and as comfortable as he could be.

Again, his thoughts drifted back to his mother. How he wished she was there at this moment to tend to his wounds. Her loving touch always had a way of making things better. She would know how to relieve the pain and clean his wounds. Just the thought of her and her caring and loving ways brought Jesus to a warm and safe place in his mind. He stayed focused on his mother for a while, thanking God for such a beautiful and wonderful soul. He could not think of another person on earth he would rather have had as his mother. It was so clear to Jesus why God had chosen her. There was no more loving and beautiful soul on the planet. Jesus prayed for his mother at that moment. In his eyes, she was not only his mother but a beacon of God's love on earth. He asked his Father in heaven to ensure that, for all generations, his mother would be remembered and regarded for these traits. He prayed that those looking for peace could find it in her and her faith in God. He prayed that all would see her as he did, as a beautiful and devoted, loving mother. He prayed that she would be a mother figure for all.

Jesus also prayed that her grace would inspire people through all generations to act as she acted, always with kindness and compassion. Her acts of charity seemed never-ending. Jesus asked his Father in heaven that she would be blessed to inspire many to embrace a life of joyful service to others. His mother was always willing to feed those in need, and she worked tirelessly to help her neighbors. Her acts of kindness and generosity were limitless, as was her love for God. Jesus knew God would have a special place in heaven for her because of the love she carried in her heart, a love for all people, and a devoted love for God. The kindness and gentle care she showed separated her from others. Jesus prayed that her grace would be remembered for all time.

Thoughts of his mother and his prayer to God helped Jesus escape the pain he was suffering from his torment for a few moments. He was lying still, and the coolness of the stone had finally overcome the heat radiating from his body. A calmness settled over him; even the trembling in his hands and within his spirit had stilled. For a fleeting moment, peace embraced him, though he knew it could not last. The reality of the situation was close to his mind, and he knew he needed to prepare for what was coming. The vision of the angry crowd yelling for him to be crucified filled his mind. He could see not only anger on their faces but hatred and fear in their hearts. Jesus knew the hearts of men, and he knew that it was because their hearts were hard that he was born. He also knew that he would die for this same reason.

His recovered sense of awareness allowed Jesus to survey the tiny room in which he was confined. The room was constructed of stone, and given the size of the stones, he could tell it was at the foundation level of the building. The stones were masterfully cut and stacked. The way they interlocked was seamless. Jesus sat and admired the work of the master stone masons. He also admired how careful and considerate they were in the cutting and placing of each stone. It was clear that it had been of importance to them to take their time and put effort into what they were doing. They had invested time and energy in mastering their skills, and it showed in their work. As Jesus looked at the walls and studied the randomness of the stones and how they fit into one another, he saw the room's completion as a representation of God's creation. He noticed that each stone was selected and shaped to fit perfectly with all the other stones. There was not one out of place. There were flat stones, like the headstone, over the door. There were large, square stones placed at ground level. They were the stones that held up the entire structure and bore its weight. There were even small stones that had been masterfully cut and placed in an arch to form the small singular window high up in the wall of this tiny room. Jesus reflected on the paradox of humanity—how man could craft such intricate structures, almost mirroring God's own creation, yet remain so distant from the divine. Jesus saw the stones as each of us, all different yet meshing to form one structure. Each was distinct in their own way, and each doing the job they were specifically chosen to do, yet they were all the same. They were all just stones, after all. As Jesus studied the walls of his cell, he noticed that the randomness of the stones wasn't random at all. He could see a pattern in what had been created in that small room. Even here, in a room built to hold criminals and thieves, there was evidence of the Almighty. "How near they are to the Father," he whispered, "and yet how distant they remain, unable to see him standing right before them."

He became frustrated at that moment. He wondered whether, if these people would just give in to God and put the same effort into his ways and his teaching, they could live their lives as well as they could stack stones. And that was the reality he faced. The fact that people would not place their faith in God was the reason he had been born. The sins of man he held in his heart became very heavy again. He was glad he was lying down, for he might have lost his balance at that moment because of the instant weight of the burden. Each sin he bore pulsed with its own sorrow and darkness, a torrent he could scarcely contain as they surged through his mind, unbidden, like a river swollen and wild. He closed his eyes, trying to keep the flood of transgressions from drowning his spirit. The flood of sins and emotion was almost overwhelming to Jesus. He took several deep breaths to calm himself and prayed to the Father for help and peace.

A psalm of David rose to his lips, a reminder of hope and deliverance:

Surely, I wait for the LORD; who bends down to me and hears my cry, draws me up from the pit of destruction, out of the muddy clay, sets my feet upon rock, steadies my steps, and puts a new song in my mouth, a hymn to our God. Many shall look on in fear and they shall trust in the LORD. Blessed the man who sets his security in the LORD, who turns not to the arrogant or to those who stray after falsehood. You, yes you, O LORD, my God, have done many wondrous deeds! And in your plans for us there is none to equal you. Should I wish to declare or tell them, too many are they to recount. Sacrifice and offering you do not want; you opened my ears. Holocaust and sin-offering you do not request; so I said, "See; I come with an inscribed scroll written upon me."

—Psalm 40:2–8

Peace came over Jesus in that moment. There was nothing more significant to him than doing the will of the Father. God wanted to free man from sin. Jesus loved everyone, as God did, and what he did was so important to them both. As Jesus prayed the words of the psalm, the Father quieted the river of thoughts and emotions Jesus experienced. Jesus felt a sense of relief as the weight of his heart was lifted by God. He gave thanks, and lying quietly, he rested, knowing they would come for him soon.

The wait was short. Jesus, caught in a peaceful meditation with God, could not tell how long he had been in the cell. All he knew was that his peace was suddenly broken by voices and footsteps outside the room. Abruptly and without warning, the wooden door was swung open with a powerful force. Two guards stood outside looking at Jesus. They had learned from experience to approach prisoners with caution. In the final hours, many men realized their fate, becoming desperate and unrestrained—driven by the terrifying freedom of having nothing left to lose. Neither of these guards was willing to risk injury by making a foolish move by rushing into the cell. They continued to stand in the doorway with their swords drawn, waiting to see if Jesus would try to force his way out of the cell to escape.

The guards were confused and distrustful of Jesus' lack of movement. They saw him lying there on the narrow stone bench in the position in which he had found comfort. The back of his tunic was soaked with blood and clinging to his body. Jesus looked tired and worn out. He did not look like a man who would give anyone much trouble, least of all the prison guards. The truth was that for the first time in hours, Jesus was comfortable, at least as comfortable as his wounds would allow. Had he been given a few more moments of peace, he might have even found it possible to sleep. Though he knew they had come to take him, a part of him resisted the summons. For once, he longed to stay here a while longer, wrapped in a fleeting sense of peace before the suffering would begin again.

The two guards kept looking at Jesus and glancing at each other. It was as if they could tell what the other was thinking without saying a word. It was as though they had an unspoken form of communication. It was clear they had done this many times before and were ready for whatever could happen. Jesus took this moment to say a silent prayer to God. He knew they would take him away, and what lay ahead on this path was more pain and suffering. "Thank you, Abba, for these few moments of rest and peace. May you be with me this day and in all that I do. May all that I do bring about your triumph and glory now and forever."

The two guards took a long last look at Jesus and turned to each other. With that, one of the prison guards lowered his sword and relaxed, with the other guard following suit. They concluded that Jesus would be no threat to them, and they were right. Jesus was just beginning to relax, and he thought to himself a few moments of sleep would have been helpful. One guard entered the room while the other stood by the door. It was his job to close the door if Jesus attacked them and tried to escape. But Jesus had no intention of escaping. He had no intention of denying the Father's glory nor letting down those he loved. It was these thoughts that gave him the resolve and courage to face the guards and whatever lay ahead. He did all this for the ones he loved, especially Abba.

The guard who entered the cell reached his hand down and grabbed Jesus by the arm. He gave a heavy-handed tug to lift Jesus off the bench. Jesus was willing to get off the bench; he just would have preferred to do so in a more thoughtful and gentle manner than the guard did. And with the jerking of his arm by the guard and his awkward stumble to get up from the bench, his tunic, which was fused to his wounds, was torn away from the skin. Jesus cried in pain. The yell did not slow down or deter the guard in any way. He continued to manhandle Jesus until he was standing upright. All this movement caused Jesus' tunic to rip open the freshly scabbed lacerations. The tunic had not completely freed itself from his back. Most of it was torn away, but he could tell it was still fused in places. It was uncomfortable and painful. With every tiny movement, he could feel the cloth tear free from another part of his flesh. It would only be a matter of time before every wound on his back was reopened.

As they walked across the cell, Jesus winced in discomfort with every footstep. With each movement, his tunic caught and tore at his wounds, scraping over freshly opened skin, the dried blood like grit between flesh and fabric. The dried blood felt like coarse sand grinding against his battered skin, each grain an abrasive reminder of his suffering. He almost wished for the final ripping just to end the torturous anticipation.

The guards led him out of his cell and down the stone hallways to a central corridor. The corridor opened into a large room with several passageways leading to it. The corridor was carefully constructed, branching into several directions with seamless efficiency. Even in this bleak moment, he noted the Romans' relentless precision, their skill apparent even in something so unfeeling as this prison. These were traits Jesus admired.

At this point, Jesus realized there was a constant flow of blood running down his back; he noticed it dripping onto the ground. He lightly touched the back of his tunic and felt that it was soaked with blood. He did not realize how badly he had been bleeding while in his cell. His back pulsed with heat, a raw reminder of the whip's brutal bite and the newly torn wounds. Every breath felt like a brush of fire against his exposed flesh. He was unsure what the exact condition of his back was, but he could tell it was in terrible shape.

Every step they took led to more pain for Jesus. The guards tried to keep a pace that Jesus could not. He wanted to move much slower. It was much easier to take slow, deliberate steps. He wanted the opportunity to ponder and give careful consideration to each stride. Jesus wanted to consider the pain and how each movement could be curtailed to keep him from wincing. The pain he was experiencing was a mental drain he could not escape. But the guards were not interested in Jesus pondering anything. They were completely without compassion for his situation or his pain. They had been given orders to collect and deliver him, and completing their task was the only thing they cared about. They were indifferent to Jesus' situation, and they forced him to move along at a speed that was less than comfortable for him.

Jesus, led by the guards, was crossing the corridor when two other guards emerged from another passageway. They yelled at the guards escorting Jesus to stop. The guards grabbed Jesus, each holding one arm as the others approached. The approaching guards advanced quickly as if they were on a mission of some importance. Their steps were quick and deliberate, and Jesus knew he was the target of their assignment. In their hands, they bore unfamiliar objects—robes of deep red and woven palms. As they approached, the glint in their eyes betrayed them. These men were no longer their own; dark spirits had overtaken their bodies, and in their hollow gaze, Jesus saw a furtherance of the torment that awaited him.

His captors ordered him to stand still while the two other guards approached. They motioned Jesus' escorts over for a conference of some sort. "You run, and you will die," one of the guards spoke into Jesus' ear.

Jesus thought about running toward one of the open hallways but did not know where it would lead. He did not think that, given his dilapidated state, it would be much of a challenge for the guards to catch him. No, this was the place and time he was supposed to be. It was here and now in this dark corridor that Jesus would face whatever was coming. It was the Father's will for him to do it, and nothing could be more critical.

As the guards continued their conversation, Jesus could tell that the guards assigned to deliver Jesus were not in favor of whatever the other two suggested. Jesus could see their furrowed brows as they continually shook their heads in disapproval. But the other guards would not give up their plea, whatever it was. They worked hard to keep the conversation alive. They stopped Jesus' guards from leaving several times to convince them that whatever their intentions were, they were worth doing. As the guards continued their conversation, their voices became louder. It was clear that neither side wanted to relent, nor did the two new guards feel that a prisoner's transportation outweighed their task.

He heard fragments of their argument, words that drifted around him like cold, lifeless air, yet he gave them little mind. Instead, his spirit grew tense as he sensed a dark presence closing in. He could see them circling the room like vultures. It was plain to see that the guards who were possessed were getting reinforcements. Two spirits came close to Jesus, their presence an icy breeze. Jesus recognized how vile these two spirits were. He thought to himself that these must be two of Satan's closest minions. These were the ones most willing and eager to please the angel of darkness. These were the spirits that helped the devil perform his most evil and destructive deeds. They were his favorites, his closest companions. Their mere essence was foul and left a stench in the air. They made him feel angry and disgusted. He kept them from getting close to him with his power. The spirits were thrown back by a force they could not see or comprehend. They became angry, and with a violent push, they threw themselves into the two guards assigned to escort Jesus.

Jesus knew that with this development, the conversation would take a different direction. Almost immediately, the two newly possessed guards stopped shaking their heads and listened to what was being described with real interest. It was clear that whatever was being discussed would be put into action soon.

At this point, Jesus prepared himself for whatever was coming. He was considering whether or not to listen intently to get the details so he would not be surprised by what was coming. It would be easy for him to learn what these men were discussing, but he decided not to. He chose to place his faith in God and simply accept his will. Jesus said a quiet prayer, "Abba, you see all things. See me and lead me to your will. May it be done here." Jesus feared to imagine what was coming next. Whatever it was, he knew it was part of his purpose. Whatever it was, it would be God's will, and that made it his will. He knew what was coming was significant, and though it might not be understood by man, it was vital for their salvation. So, he allowed it to begin.

Suddenly, the debate ended. The four men fell silent, their faces shifting as a single, sinister intent filled their gaze. Jesus looked back, but he no longer saw merely human faces. Through the masks of flesh, he saw the spirits controlling them, their influence snaking through each guard's eyes like dark clouds blotting out the light. With that, he held these men harmless from whatever wrongdoing was about to happen. He surveyed his tormentors, for that was their intended purpose, to torment him. There was no question about that. They looked half-crazed, and two of them had smiles on their faces.

Among the dark spirits surrounding him, one was particularly familiar—a figure steeped in bitterness and pride. This one did not mock with the others. Instead, his gaze was cold, a simmering hatred glinting behind his eyes. It was clear this spirit felt slighted by Jesus, wounded by the force that had once driven him back. He hovered with a quiet, dangerous intensity like an adversary waiting for the moment to reclaim his power.

Evidently, when Jesus had forced the spirits away from getting close to him, it caused them some sort of discomfort or pain, and this spirit was looking to get back at Jesus.

Though this group looked ready to kill a wild beast with their bare hands and tear off pieces of its flesh to devour it raw, they did not immediately approach Jesus. Jesus stood there waiting for the oncoming misery, and a feeling of cold and emptiness came upon him. Those feelings were familiar to Jesus, and he knew the devil was near.

"What do you want?" asked Jesus?

"Son of Man, you have taken something from me, and I want it returned," said the devil.

"I have nothing but what the Father has given to me, and if He has given it, then whatever it is could not have been yours. One cannot give away what one does not have," explained Jesus.

The devil's voice rose, a twisted howl of defiance. "You enter my realm, daring to disrupt the order I have shaped, twisting the truth itself. Sin is my dominion! Man's transgressions belong to me—I have ruled them since they were first brought forth by man!" Jesus quietly responded, "I am the way, the truth, and the life. Whoever comes to me comes to my Father. That is the way of things. It is not the false promises you make."

The devil's voice lowered, dripping with a twisted imitation of reason. "Listen, Jesus of Nazareth," he sneered, "these are my most devoted servants. Whatever I command, they obey without question. I need only will it, and they will grant you mercy—or unleash pain beyond what flesh can bear. Lay down this burden; cast off the sins you carry, and I will restrain them."

Jesus looked at the devil and said, "Blessed am I to carry the burden of the Lord. I am loyal and subject to his will, for his will is my will. It is out of love that I do this, and love will triumph on this day. This is the day of the Lord. On this day, salvation will triumph. So do as you will, but understand I could no more put down the sins of man than I could deny myself of who I am, one with the Father. His will be done on earth as it is in heaven. The days of darkness are over."

Jesus' commitment to his task and his clear contempt for the devil's authority drove the evil one into a rage-filled convulsion. His hatred and anger boiled over into a wave of darkness never seen before by man. Jesus watched as the devil boiled in a fit of anger. He frightened his minions, and they trembled at his rage.

In a last, desperate attempt to get Jesus to release the sins of man from his heart, the devil wildly approached Jesus. "I have the power to control the hearts and thoughts of men. This is my domain, and if I will it, you can become a king. If I will it, you could be torn down by those whom you love so much. You know that I am right in what I say. Give me what I want, and I will make you the prince of the earth."

Jesus intently looked at the devil and said, "You have nothing to give, you only take. You take from these the truth, and you hide it to fool them. You offer nothing but lies, despair, and destruction. As I said, do you not realize that you cannot give away what you do not have? Do you not realize that the Kingdom of God is at hand? You would make me a prince of what, darkness? I am the way, the truth, and the life, as I have told you before. Whoever comes to me will see the Kingdom of heaven. This is my domain."

Realizing that Jesus, even though beaten and abused by them, loved the people so much that there was nothing the devil could do or say to have him release man's sins, the devil relented. "So, you seek to reign over heaven and earth? To claim authority over the sins of humanity and accomplish this supposed salvation? Very well. Let it be so—I will ensure you feel the full weight of this crown you have claimed."

With that, the four possessed guards approached Jesus. As they reached him, they grabbed his tunic and tore it off his body as quickly as they could. As they removed his clothing, the freshly scabbed wounds on his back were again torn open, and now many were oozing. Yet again, he felt blood running down his back. Jesus arched and gasped in pain. The guards had no mercy on him, nor did they care about his condition. They worked along, completely ignoring Jesus' exasperation at the pain and agony.

After some time, the guards had managed to get Jesus out of his tunic and into a guard's robe. They draped a crimson robe over his shoulders—a mockery of royalty, the deep color bordering on purple, meant to scorn the dignity it signified. Jesus felt the coarse fabric scrape painfully against his raw wounds, but he bore the humiliation with silent grace. Pleased with their work, they led him out into the vast courtyard.

Only a few soldiers in the courtyard saw what was happening, but they called on others to join them. Soon, the courtyard became filled with more soldiers. It was as though none of them wanted to miss the day's events. They all gathered around to laugh and make fun of Jesus. Jesus looked at the ever-growing crowd and felt embarrassed. How must I look? He thought to himself.

He paused, his gaze sweeping over the crowd. A heavy, almost tangible darkness simmered in the air, a wave of hardened hearts and eyes that refused to see. It struck him how alone he felt, how his spirit was so different from these men, whose faith had withered into mere shadows. How nice it would be to be surrounded by his friends to comfort him. But he knew if they were there, they would suffer the same fate as him. This was not their day, not their time. It was his. For the Father, they would all face trials and triumphs in their own way. Still, he thought of Peter and his brothers, and a sort of peace came upon him again. He would endure this ridicule for them and all whom he loved. Jesus was unsure exactly what was going to happen because he chose not to know, but he knew it would happen for a reason. So, for the Father's glory and for the ones he loved, he would endure this insufferable situation.

One of the guards approached Jesus and thrust a reed into his hand. The guard cried out so all could hear him, "You cannot be king without a scepter of power!" The entire group laughed. Then the four circled Jesus, looking at him intently, trying to judge whether he looked kingly. "We have missed something—something important," said one of the guards. "He cannot be a king without a crown!" he turned and shouted with theatrical flourish, he retrieved a crown—woven not of laurels or jewels but of thorns, fierce and unforgiving. The thorns on the crown protruded out in every direction. It was as if hate itself had been woven into a band. There was not a place on the crown without long, sharp thorns protruding out. The guard who was approaching Jesus yelped in pain continually as the thorns pricked his fingers. He carried the crown lightly as if he had just pulled it from a fire and was trying not to get burned by it. Jesus felt a wave of dread rise within him, an ache deep and unfamiliar. In all his years, such dread had scarcely touched him, but now it seemed to linger like a shadow, a constant companion in these final hours. Yet he remained steady, his resolve firm even as the guard raised the crown with a twisted smile, ready to press it down onto his brow.

The guard stood before Jesus, holding the thorned crown aloft as the other guards took their places, encircling him. Suddenly, a voice slithered into Jesus' mind, soft but sinister—the voice of the devil himself, whispering, "A king you desire to be, so a king I shall make you." The soldiers sank to one knee in mocking reverence, their half-smiles twisted into masks of dark glee. This, after all, was a king's coronation, and decorum demanded a show of respect—no matter how laced with contempt. The guards all had half smiles on their crazed faces. One of the guards gingerly held the thorny crown over Jesus' head and exclaimed, "Here on this day I crown you, the king of the Jews." He placed the crown on Jesus' head. Instantly, the sharp points of the thorns cut into his scalp. The three guards kneeling before Jesus began to chant, "All hail the king of the Jews . . . all hail the king of the Jews." Their voices rose and fell in a sickening rhythm, and soon, the entire assembly joined, their jeers reverberating like a twisted hymn through the air. As if the humiliation of the situation wasn't enough for Jesus, it also was extremely painful. The guard who had crowned Jesus removed his sword and, using the handle, pressed the crown of thorns deep into Jesus' scalp. Jesus yelled out in pain, and with that, the crowd began to yell and cheer. Seeing the pain on Jesus' face brought them much joy. He had become a spectacle for their entertainment.

Jesus became angry and frustrated. He did not enjoy being the brunt of this cruel and blasphemous joke. He was tired to the point of exhaustion. He was tired of the mockery. He was angry that these men, with hearts so dark, were ridiculing him and the Father. He wanted to lash out and release himself from this humiliation, and with that feeling, the sins in his heart began to burn. A wave of dark emotion ran through him like a gale from the sea. He knew these emotions were not his. They were from what he carried in his heart. The sins of man could sense the desire of Jesus to use his power. And if there was anything that appealed to man, it was power, and Jesus' power knew no limits. It seemed the sins were encouraging Jesus to use the power he had to release himself. In some way, it seemed like they would be enriched by that act of selfishness. It was then he understood why the devil craved the sins of men so deeply—this was the source, the root of his dark influence. Without them, the devil would be powerless, stripped of the very fuel he used to tear souls away from the light.

With this new realization, a tear formed in Jesus' eye. He looked around at the group of yelling and chanting soldiers, and compassion spilled out of him like a heavy rain. He saw how lost these men were and how much they needed salvation. He thought of the ones whom he loved and knew this was a significant moment for them all. Here and now, in front of hate itself, he would lock away the sins of man forever in his heart, his human heart. In that instant, something within him changed. His heart began to harden, but not as an ordinary heart hardens. When a human heart hardens, it closes, fortified by fear and anger, keeping everything out—even love. But as Jesus' heart took on this new strength, it opened to receive all things, never to release them. He would carry it all—not only love but every sin. His heart would still know suffering, still be capable of breaking, yet it would hold steadfastly to what he bore. For the sake of mankind, he would carry this burden. Jesus decided to keep these sins close to him. "Forever, they will be mine," he whispered, "for how can people be saved and lifted to heaven with such a burden on their souls?"

With this miraculous transformation, Jesus also noticed that carrying the sins of men went from being a burden to a joy. They no longer weighed him down. The weight lifted, and even amid ridicule, pain, and mockery, he felt light and freed. Jesus saw the importance of this moment and wondered if the people would be able see the wisdom of the Father through the pain they felt in life. He prayed quietly that in their own suffering, they might find His love.

Realizing the transformation within Jesus' heart, the devil felt a new surge of rage. He had lost the sins of humanity forever, for he understood now that Jesus would guard them with an unwavering hold. Furious, he longed to retaliate, to punish Jesus for taking what he saw as rightfully his. But with each passing moment, the devil's power was draining away. He sensed that soon he would be confined to the shadows, relegated to subtlety and whispers. The time of his direct assaults on human souls would come to an end, and his reach over the pure-hearted would weaken. He would be left only to torment the frail and the fallen—those already vulnerable to his influence. But where was the challenge, the satisfaction, in that? The wicked already belonged to him, and the weak offered little resistance. For so long, he had relished in tormenting even the most faithful, watching their struggles under his influence. Now, that terrible pleasure was slipping from his grasp. However, now, with Jesus' reigning over the sins of man, the devil would not be able to enrich himself from these sins. From this day on, he would be limited to preying on the weakness of man through temptation. He would never be able to use his power to force people to rebel against God and their own will.

The devil felt himself weakening as though part of his very being was slipping away. A desire flared within him to seize control of this frenzied mob, to rend Jesus apart with his own hands if he could. Yet, bitterly, he realized his influence had waned; he could no longer wield direct power over the strong. But he could still work through the frail and the corrupt. He noticed his four trusted servants still had full control of the men they possessed. "I will get my revenge with the weak," the devil said. With a sinister intensity, he turned his focus back to the guards and commanded, "If he insists on being crowned as king of sin, let him know the weight of that crown. Make him feel the sting, for the sins of man are sharp and cut deeply." I want him to feel their sting!" With that, the guard grabbed the thick reed out of Jesus' hand and hit him violently on his head. With every blow, the thorns in the crown were driven deeper and deeper. Jesus screamed in pain as an exceptionally long and sharp thorn pierced deep into the side of his skull.

These new actions led the crowd to cheer and mock him by shouting out, "All hail the king of the Jews!" Every time the guards yelled out, it was followed by great laughter. The guards were now taking turns smacking Jesus on the head with the reed. They had also started to spit at him. Jesus found this to be extremely humiliating, but for now, he had the deepest desire for them to stop hitting the crown of thorns. It had been Jesus' hope to remove the crown after the mockery was over. The problem was, he knew now it had become so deeply embedded into his skin and mangled in his hair that he doubted it could ever be removed.

The blood from the thorns embedded in his scalp streamed down, mingling with the sweat that trickled through his hair—a mixture born of relentless pain and open wounds. Blood ran down his forehead and into his eyes. His eyes were tearing up from the sting of sweat and blood that kept running into them, and Jesus was having trouble focusing. He had to keep wiping his eyes to keep them clear, and this caused yet more discomfort, for his new clothes had soaked up the blood from his back wounds and stuck to his open flesh as it dried. Every time Jesus lifted his arm to wipe his eyes, the cloth ripped free from his skin and painfully reopened the old wounds. Every movement became an agony of blood and exposed flesh, yet he bore it quietly, his spirit lifting in silent prayer. "Abba," he prayed, "I see your wisdom, and I have held secure what you entrusted to me. Please, release me from this. I have done all you asked."

In that moment, the guard holding the reed faltered, his grasp loosening as if unseen chains fell from his soul, and the dark spirit that had gripped him withdrew.

As all four spirits were driven out of their hosts, the men looked at one another, confused and surprised. They all knew they were responsible for what had just happened, but they were unsure how and why it had taken place. The head guard cleared his throat and loudly announced, "The show is over!" A wave of boos and hisses erupted from the crowd, but slowly, the spectators dispersed, their mocking laughter echoing faintly as they left. From a distance, Jesus could still hear guards jeering, "All hail the king of the Jews!" as they wandered off, their voices fading into the distance. Without a word, the two guards assigned to escort Jesus took him by the arm. They led him out of the large courtyard and back down the stone path. Their demeanor was much different as they led him out of the area than when they had led him in. On the way in, they had not cared how much discomfort he was in or the level of pain they might be causing. His escorts, on the way out, guided him gently, no longer pushing or prodding. They seemed to feel pity for him and what they had done. They allowed Jesus to walk at his own pace. Jesus could see the compassion they had in their eyes, and he thought to himself, how could I hold this against them? They are like children, blind to the full weight of their actions. With quiet forgiveness, he resolved today, their sins are forgiven.

Jesus and the guards returned down the stone hallway as the devil retreated. The devil could feel himself getting weaker and weaker by the moment. He was beginning to realize to what extent Jesus had reduced his authority over men. The devil understood it would only be a matter of time before vast numbers of people would come to believe in Jesus and give their lives to God. Fury coursed through him, a rage so profound it nearly consumed him. He realized he could no longer torment or mock the Son of Man, and yet, amidst his frustration, he clung to one small comfort: Jesus' suffering was not yet complete.

"The crown of thorns is a profound paradox. The King of all is crowned with suffering, yet through that very suffering, He reigns victorious over sin and death."

—Venerable Fulton J. Sheen

CHAPTER 4

The Cross

— • • —

Jesus was taken back to the spot where he had been dressed in the red soldier's uniform. He looked down at the ground and saw his own clothes lying there. He knew he would need to remove the uniform he was wearing and put his clothing back on. He took a deep breath and let out a long sigh. He tried to mentally prepare himself for the oncoming discomfort and pain of changing his clothes. With much more care and compassion than they had displayed originally, the guards helped Jesus out of the uniform and back into his tunic. The process was painful and slow. Jesus took each step in a careful and calculated manner. He was grateful the guards did not rush him. With every movement Jesus made, the pain was clear on his face. The guards aided him in removing the uniform and redressed him in his blood-soaked tunic. They made every effort to avoid the crown that was lodged in his skull and tangled in his hair. Nonetheless, twice, his clothes caught the crown of thorns as he dressed.

The rough, blood-soaked fabric of his tunic clung painfully to his raw skin, each fiber like sandpaper scraping against open wounds. Every shift of the coarse material was an assault, as if he wore not a tunic but a jagged coat of stone. The only relief came from the sickening mix of blood and pus that oozed from his lacerations, offering some lubrication to the otherwise brutal, stiff cloth. He was very aware of the injuries he had sustained. His back was once again on fire, and his head had a mixture of sharp, stabbing pains and aches. The long-pointed thorns caused the stabbing pain. When Jesus moved his head, he was careful. He could feel the thorns rip deeper into his skin when he moved too quickly. Parts of his head also felt like they were swelling greatly. He was unsure how many times he had been hit with the reed, but the pain that was inflicted with each blow had turned into one massive ache.

At this point, the blood running from his head slowed, and he did not have to wipe his eyes as much. Jesus was thankful for these simple favors. His eyes were stinging, but wiping them only caused more irritation. His head hurt so much that he found it challenging to focus on objects at a distance. He stared at the ground. He didn't know why—it just seemed easier. Jesus wanted to look up, but he felt like looking up meant looking ahead, and he was not looking forward to what was coming. For now, he would not look ahead. He would not rush into the future but meet it as it arrived, step by step. He knew well that worrying about what was to come served no purpose. He was in the Father's hands, and the road would unfold as it was meant to. With quiet resolve, he recommitted himself to the task before him, trusting that peace and strength would return in their own time when the Father willed it.

The two guards stood there watching Jesus. He had closed his eyes and appeared to be meditating. They were trying to get Jesus to his next destination, and they were running later than they should have been. Even so, neither dared to interrupt him. There was something vastly different and amazing about the state he seemed to be in. It felt as if disturbing him at this moment would be like disturbing the sun from shining or the sea from creating waves. It would have been an abomination in some way. In his presence, the guards found themselves rooted in silence, unable to break the stillness that enveloped them. Slowly, they ceased to be merely his captors. In that sacred moment, they became his silent keepers, his guardians. Without words or command, they would have stopped anyone who dared approach him, sensing the holiness of the moment they were witnessing.

After several minutes, Jesus felt at peace again. He had found a way to be calm and peaceful despite the wounds and the crown of thorns fused to his head. He had found a way to be peaceful even though the future held more torment and pain. Jesus accepted everything he had been handed. He knew it was for a reason—and the reason was man. He thought of the ancient prophets, of their words, and how, through them, the destiny of the Son of Man had been foretold. Now, that destiny was unfolding before him. The prophecies had been written, and now, they were being fulfilled. A quiet joy filled him, a fleeting moment of happiness for the fulfillment of what had been long promised. In his mind's eye, he recalled the righteous men and women who had come before him, those who had walked in faith and knew that they, too, would now enter the Kingdom of Heaven. While he covered his heart with his hand, his thoughts flashed through the ages. The sins of man helped Jesus to picture all of those whom he loved in the past, present, and future. They helped because all men had sinned, but Jesus loved them all anyway, as the Father did. As tired as he was and as much as he hurt, how could he not complete this task? His actions would lead so many wonderful people into his Father's glorious kingdom. He knew there was no real choice, and he took satisfaction in knowing that these moments of sacrifice would not only save the souls of those who had already died but they would also save so many for generations to come. He knew his example of suffering for the will of God would be repeated many times and lead countless numbers to salvation.

After taking those few moments to enjoy a sense of renewed peace, Jesus opened his eyes. Without speaking a word, he nodded to his escorts, motioning that he was ready to proceed. This time, his captors were different. There was no pushing or prodding from them. They quietly moved Jesus down the stone passageway with dignity. The two of them still felt Jesus' connection with the Father. They did not understand or even realize what had happened, but they were unknowingly affected by it. They had transformed from leading him as a prisoner to escorting him as a man of significant importance traveling to a state affair. They became sentries of his protection, not guards preventing his escape. The guards knew that for Jesus, this had become his quest. There was no escaping from what was to come.

One stone passageway led to the next, and after a series of turns and twists along the route, they emerged from the building. As the last corridor brought them into an extremely bright opening, Jesus squinted his eyes. The sun was getting higher in the sky, and the day was beginning to heat up. It took a minute for his eyes to adjust. As the group made their way across the courtyard, all those who were in the area stopped to watch as Jesus walked by. The conversation became frozen as their eyes followed Jesus from one side of the courtyard to the other. They were all aware that this was a man who was heading for his death. His appearance was horrible. His clothes were dirty and soaked in blood. His hair was matted from a combination of sweat, dirt, and blood. The crown of thorns was wrapped around his head and entangled in his hair. His face was swollen from the beatings and covered in blood and bruises. He was almost unrecognizable, but it was not his condition that made people stare. It was the look on his face and the determination in the way he walked. As they gazed at him, it was like following the flight of a butterfly. The combination of pain and fatigue left Jesus' steps uneasy and random, but yet also clear and purposeful.

Just as a butterfly's erratic flight can be mesmerizing in its grace and intent, so was Jesus' walk through the courtyard. Despite the brutality he had endured, there was a beauty to his suffering. His path was as clear as it was inevitable. And like the butterfly, he captured the attention of all those around him. The courtyard fell into a heavy silence, all eyes fixed on him as he passed, his every movement speaking of something far greater than what the eye could see.

Jesus had a resonant sense of determination. His stride, which was still somewhat broken and fragmented, gained momentum as he walked across the courtyard. He made his way to the building on the other side. The door was open, and Jesus headed in. He knew he would soon be given his cross for crucifixion. All this time, the voices of the crowd that had rung out at Pilate's hearing were ever-present in his mind. "Crucify him! Crucify him!" Jesus listened to the chant replay in his head over and over as he walked. The vision of hate and anger on the faces of those who cried out for his demise was clear in his mind. And again, he became very aware of the sins of man in his heart. It was people not loving God the Father that bothered him the most. He was very aware that his actions this day would lead to the salvation of many, but not of all. He thought of this sacrifice and felt hurt that some would always reject him and the Father. This thought made Jesus incredibly sad, but it also reinforced his commitment to the mission ahead. Yet, he pressed on, for love—true love—was the only force strong enough to carry him through this trial.

Jesus could see a collection of crosses on the other side of the room. He was led to a group of guards there, where they waited for him. A conversation broke out among the guards, but Jesus did not pay attention to the discussion. He walked over and viewed the selection of crosses. He had seen people hang on a cross before and was aware of the pain he was about to suffer. Having been trained as a carpenter by his earthly father, Joseph, Jesus viewed the crosses from that perspective. His hand moved over the rough wood of one of the crosses, feeling the grain, noticing the imperfections. The tool marks were uneven, the edges jagged. He could tell at once that the blade used to shape the wood had not been properly maintained—dull and worn, it had left behind splinters where clean cuts should have been. The unfinished strokes had torn at the wood rather than sliced through it, a mark of a craftsman who either lacked skill or simply did not care enough to sharpen his tools. A skilled carpenter, Jesus thought, would have taken the time to keep his tools in shape, knowing that dull blades only lead to inefficiency and wasted effort. Looking at the joint where the pieces of wood met, Jesus saw the same signs of inexperience. The cut was crooked, the depth inconsistent, and the gap at the upper left side of the joint was too wide. The joints should have fit together with precision, a testament to the care and expertise of the craftsman. But this was not the work of someone who took pride in their craft. Whether out of haste or negligence, the poor workmanship was undeniable. Jesus felt a momentary pang of sadness—not for the crosses themselves, but for the wasted potential of a craft so integral to human life, a life now marked by so much carelessness.

Jesus, thinking back to all the lessons and skills given to him by his earthly father, would never have dared to bring a piece of work so poorly cut to his attention. He thought about how Joseph had taught him the carpentry trade. A smile came to his face as his hand caressed the rough wood grain. Jesus remembered as a young man how so many pieces of work were given back to him because they were too rough. "The wood must be smooth to the touch," Joseph would say to him. "If you are going to do something, do it well and finish what you start." This was another favorite saying of his earthly father. Jesus thought about how much pride Joseph took in his craft. He treated it as the true gift it really was. Jesus knew it made his earthly father happy to create things. It pleased him so much to take a raw piece of wood and turn it into something beautiful and useful. Jesus marveled at how his Father God was the same way. He would take someone who was rough but raw with potential and turn them into a beacon of love and light for others. As Joseph used a chisel to chop away the wood not needed to make his project perfectly crafted, God would also chisel away at the things that made people less than perfect. Jesus was thinking about Joseph working away in his shop. He noticed that his hammer sometimes hit the chisel with great force to eliminate large pieces of unneeded wood. God would do the same to the ones he loved. Jesus understood the significance of this process—how, at times, suffering and refinement were inextricably linked. He wished, with all his heart, that people would come to see that the pain they endured was not meaningless. He hoped they would understand that it was through their suffering, their trials, that they would become more perfect, more capable of loving and living as they were meant to. His own suffering this day was part of that greater plan, a sacrifice not just for the people of his time but for all people—so that they might one day find the fullness of love, peace, and salvation.

Jesus saw so many similarities between Joseph, his earthly father, and Abba, his Heavenly one. Jesus understood why God had chosen Joseph to take care of his only son. He was a man of dignity and respect, and he loved his family and work. Jesus thought of God and how he enjoyed creating the heavens and the earth, as well as that glorious moment when God created man and how much God loved his creation. Joseph also cherished his little family. Jesus realized that God was not the only one giving up a son on this day. His heart, which was already full, opened to Joseph. He knew that the events that were about to take place would hurt his earthly father greatly. No father would want to see their son suffer. Jesus hoped, with all his heart, that Joseph would be proud of him, proud of the path he had chosen to walk. Though Joseph had long since passed, Jesus trusted that his heavenly

Father had already welcomed him into glory. The thought that Joseph would one day be exalted in heaven brought Jesus peace. He knew that his father's obedience and unwavering faith would be remembered by all, not just as a legacy of love but as an example of devotion that transcended even death itself.

A faint smile touched Jesus' lips as he recalled the voice of Joseph in his mind: It's not ready until it's smooth, son. This was the essence of his mission—to smooth the jagged edges of salvation, to make a rough path ready for all to walk. He knew he would have to finish what was started today. He felt the rough surface of the cross again and closed his eyes to picture Joseph one last time. He knew it would take a tremendous amount of focus to complete what lay ahead of him. He did not want to miss this one last opportunity to give thanks and pay homage to the man who had cared for him here on the earth.

"Ah, it seems you've made your choice," a voice called from across the room, its tone heavy with mockery. Jesus turned his gaze toward the men, who watched him with indifferent eyes. "Good choice," one of them added, followed by a harsh laugh that reverberated through the air like a cruel echo.

The two guards who had brought Jesus to this place stood in silence for a moment, their eyes avoiding the scene before them. The weight of what had been done hung between them, yet they had fulfilled their duty. Jesus had been handed over to those who would carry out the next part of his ordeal. Their job was done. Without a word, they turned, their footsteps echoing as they walked away from the suffering they had helped deliver.

"Not sticking around?" the mocking voice of the guard called out behind them. But the two did not respond; their departure marked the end of their involvement in the pain that would unfold.

The guards who were departing stopped and turned slightly to look at each other. Again, in unspoken communication, they nodded to one another, moved back toward the door, and left quickly. The remaining guards looked at each other in a puzzled manner, unsure why their comrades had left with such haste. After a series of glances back and forth, they shrugged their shoulders then turned their focus on Jesus.

Jesus still stood with one hand on the cross in front of him, mostly for support at this point, and he looked at his newly appointed captors with dread. He knew these men were cruel and enjoyed being that way. He was not looking forward to the next step, but there was no reason to delay. That would only prolong the suffering, and Jesus was ready to move on. The head guard stepped forward, his voice sharp and laced with mockery. "Well, if you're so fond of that one," he sneered, motioning toward the cross, "then take it and let's get moving." The command was delivered coldly, without empathy, as though his words were as sharp as the cross itself.

Jesus sized up the cross, then wrapped his hands around it. He gave it a tug to stand it upright, and when he did, some of the wounds on his back ripped open again. He steadied the cross as he winced in pain. For a few moments, he forgot about his back. The pain wasn't eliminated; he was just becoming accustomed to it. As the cross scraped against his raw flesh, the reopening of his wounds sent a fresh wave of agony through Jesus' body. For a fleeting moment, he tried to steady his breath, willing the burning pain to subside. But the moment of relief was short-lived. The guard, growing impatient, struck him harshly with the whip. "Move it—this can't take all day!" he barked, the crack of the lash echoing through the air.

The heat of the whip surged like fire across Jesus' back, radiating outward, causing every muscle to tense. His face flushed with the intensity, his pulse throbbing violently in his temples. Each beat of his heart intensified the pressure in his skull, the thorns digging deeper into his flesh, sending waves of blinding pain. He knew he had no choice but to continue moving—if he didn't, the guard's whip would strike again.

The guard understood that most condemned men did not want to carry a cross to their death. He also understood that it would take a lot of discomfort to motivate them to pick up the cross and walk. Jesus did not need this motivation. He knew this was his mission here on the earth, and he certainly had been whipped enough for one day. He had already accepted the fact that he was going to die, and he wanted to keep the pain to a minimum if possible. He was prepared to carry this cross to his death.

Jesus turned to get under the cross and slowly eased it onto his shoulders. But the cross was top-heavy, and it came down faster than Jesus was prepared for. As the cross hit his shoulder heavily, Jesus felt his knees start to give way. He caught himself before they collapsed and pushed his legs and back upright. He felt the cross come to rest on his back. This was the very thing he had been trying to avoid. He really didn't want this heavy cross resting on his back and rubbing against his wounds for the entire journey, as it caused severe pain. He was unsure if he wanted to walk or reposition the cross to ease the discomfort. Every step forward seemed to bring a new wave of suffering. The agony from the cross rubbing against his body was unbearable, and he knew that neither walking nor repositioning it would bring relief. Both paths promised only more pain. As he wrestled with this, the whip cracked again, its sting landing squarely on the cross. Jesus wasn't sure if it was a careless mistake from the guard or divine intervention, but in that moment, he felt a deep sense of gratitude.

"Get going!" the guard shouted. And with that command, Jesus slowly began his painful journey, one deliberate step at a time, toward Golgotha.

Jesus followed one of the guards out the door and onto the path that would lead to his death. The cross was heavy and a real burden for someone as tired and fatigued as Jesus. He fought between two thoughts. He wondered which would cause him to stop first: the immense pain caused by the cross resting and rubbing the wounds on his back or the weakness in his knees. He found himself breathing hard after only a few short steps and wondered how he could make the entire journey. He decided to focus on the task at hand. He would try to replace pain with understanding and comprehension. If you understand something, even if it is painful, it's easier to bear, he thought to himself. He allowed his mind to focus on God and man, knowing he was the link between the two. He was attempting to figure out why the Father had chosen this method of death and how this would all help the salvation of mankind. Despite his efforts, his thoughts often slipped away from the profound, drawn back to the weight of the cross that pressed mercilessly against him. Each step was a test of endurance, each moment stretching into eternity. He couldn't even pay attention to where he was walking. He stared down at his feet, almost as if he had to concentrate to force each one to take the next step. In his mind, he remained determined to make it to the end. Ultimately, Jesus found peace in the knowledge that this suffering was the Father's will, and in accepting that, it became His own. There was comfort in this surrender, knowing that God would never burden Him beyond His strength—even if, at times, the weight felt unbearable. Jesus continued on the path, which was beginning to be lined with people. It did not take long for word to get out that Jesus was carrying a cross and was heading toward Golgotha. People were in a hurry to line up to see him. The path that condemned people took to Golgotha was well-known to them. They had seen the Romans march many men along this route to their deaths. The path was filled with all kinds of people for varied reasons. Some came out in support of Jesus. They found him to be a man too kind to deserve this kind of death. In fact, they did not feel he deserved to die at all. There were other people who came out in anticipation of some remarkable spectacle that might take place. In their doubt, they laughed and mocked him as he passed by. In their hearts, they did not believe he was the Son of God, and they could not understand what he was trying to accomplish. As Jesus struggled under the weight of the cross, the crowd jeered and mocked him. They laughed and pointed, cruelly taking pleasure in his suffering. Every moan of pain that escaped his lips was met with scornful jest. The rough timber of the cross scraped painfully against his raw skin, aggravating the wounds on his back, and he could feel the blood seeping from them, adding to the torment.

However, among the crowd also were the faithful, those who believed. These were the ones who shared Jesus' love. He could hear them weeping as he passed by. The sounds of their grief tore through his mind as his heart broke for them. As he heard their cries and saw their tears, he wished he could put this cross down and console them. Through the entire crowd, a young girl's tears caught his eye. He saw her weeping for him, and he was moved by deep compassion. Jesus could tell this girl was pure of heart and loved with her entire soul. Jesus could see the love of God she had and how it lit her up from the inside out. Jesus was completely taken by her love, and his heart broke over her sadness. He tried to maintain his focus on her as he moved forward, but the unbearable weight of the cross caused him to lose his balance. His right foot gave way, and the burden was too heavy to bear. Jesus staggered, then collapsed onto the ground. He released the cross and reached out instinctively, his hands bracing for the fall. His palms met the earth first, followed by the painful crash of his chest.

This fall, even in his weakened state, ordinarily would not have been all that much for him to handle, but this day, it would not be so easy. As his chest collided with the earth, the cross's significant weight pressed down upon him, crushing the breath from his lungs. He gasped for air, but the cross lifted briefly before slamming down once more, its sharp edges digging painfully into his already battered back. This time, the cross slid across his head, driving the crown of thorns even deeper. Jesus yelled in excruciating pain. At the same time, he could hear the screams and sobs from those who loved him. In addition, he could hear laughter and cheers from those who mocked him.

Jesus lay on the ground, his body writhing in pain. The weight of the cross pressed down on him, holding him in place. He closed his eyes while gathering himself internally. He understood this was just the start of his journey; he had a long way to go. If he was going to make it, it would take all his strength and more. When he felt he could focus his energy away from the pain and back on his task, he opened his eyes. He looked at the crowd from ground level. He could see the feet of many people. His falling had caused many to gather nearby. A sense of humiliation washed over Jesus as he lay there, sprawled in the dirt. The laughter of the crowd echoed in his ears, and he felt the sting of their mockery. This was not the image he wished to leave behind. He had walked a path of righteousness, a path meant to lead others to salvation, yet here he was, covered in the dust of the earth, vulnerable and shamed. The purity of his mission seemed clouded in that moment as if the message of love and grace was lost in the mockery.

As Jesus looked back at the growing crowd of people, he did not get up immediately. Some of his followers got down on their hands and knees to check if he was okay. He looked at their faces and saw tears in their eyes. It caused them pain to see him like this. Jesus felt a sense of defeat at this moment. After all, he was doing all this out of love for them. And here were the ones he loved so much, pouring every ounce of love from their hearts into his. They were there to give him strength and support, and he was there to give them salvation, though they did not realize it. As he drew strength from the ones he loved, he decided to get up and keep moving. It was about that same time that the guards shared a similar thought. The moment Jesus fell to the ground, the guards' harsh voices pierced through the chaos, demanding that he rise. At first, their shouts seemed distant, almost muffled, but as he lay there, they grew nearer and more insistent. Their patience had worn thin, and now their commands cut through him with force. There was no more mercy in their tone, no more space for hesitation—just the cold urgency of their authority.

With no warning, Jesus felt the sting of the whip once again. One of the guards was screaming at him at this point, threatening to whip him even more if he didn't get up and keep moving. Jesus was tired of being whipped. From a deep desire not to have it happen again, he buried the pain and tried to get up off the ground.

Rising from the ground was a Herculean task. Every muscle screamed in protest as the sharp throb of pain coursed through his body, each beat of his heart amplifying the agony in his skull. Yet, despite the unbearable weight of the moment, the relentless sting of the whip drove him forward. With unwavering resolve, he reached down to lift the cross, knowing it was his only path forward. As Jesus bent over, the throbbing in his head intensified. When he grabbed his cross and lifted it, the pain intensified to another level. He knew he needed to get the cross picked up quickly, or he would pass out from the pain. The cross seemed to have gained weight in the fall. The cross felt impossibly heavy, its weight pressing down on him with an intensity that surpassed anything he had felt before. Each step seemed to increase its burden as if the very essence of his suffering was bound to its mass. He became dreadfully aware of his fatigue and realized that the fall had done real damage to his strength.

Jesus managed to lift the cross off the ground, but he struggled to get it back onto his shoulder. The cross was unsteady in his hand, and it felt like he was losing control of it. The guard's action was not born of mercy or kindness but rather an instinctive reflex. As Jesus faltered once more, the cross threatening to slip from his grasp, the guard reached out without hesitation, his hand steadying the burden—no thought of compassion, only the reflex to prevent another fall or to have it fall on him. Jesus knew it was not kindness that led the soldier to help, but he was thankful anyway. Now, with the cross securely positioned against his body, Jesus continued on his way.

With these first few steps, cheers could be heard from those who made fun of Jesus. It was as if their amusement could continue, and they were happy the show would go on. Jesus could see this had infuriated some of the sobbing women. They turned to yell at and scold those men who had made a joke out of Jesus' pain. Jesus almost felt a smile to come to his face. Had it not been for the extreme pain he was in; he was sure he would have been smiling from ear to ear. The thought of those little old ladies scolding those men and making them feel like young boys in trouble made Jesus laugh on the inside. He thought to himself, oh, how faith truly emboldens the meek.

As Jesus looked at the path ahead of him, the warm feeling quickly was replaced by the reality of the distance he would have to cover in order to get to his destination. It was an exceptionally long way yet to Golgotha.

Jesus slowly and painfully continued his journey. The path ahead of him was easily defined by people lining the way. As Jesus made his way forward, a multitude longed to rush toward him, yearning to touch the source of the miracles they had witnessed. Each of them knew that the simple grace of his touch had been a blessing, and now, in the shadow of what was to come, they clung to the hope of one last blessing. This, they imagined, would be their final opportunity to reach out for such divine favor. At times, the guards who escorted Jesus were quite busy keeping the crowd away from him. The people would press in on him in a desperate attempt to receive his touch. The guards violently pushed them back and whipped those in the forefront of the crowd. Jesus watched as the guards threatened to put many on the crucifixion line with Jesus if they didn't stay back. Jesus knew what they were after and thought in his mind If they only knew the gifts they will receive after I am finished.

Jesus dropped his eyes away from the people lining the path in front of him. He grew weary of meeting their eyes. It was simpler to fix his gaze on the ground beneath him. In doing so, he could shield himself from confronting the selfishness of those gathered around him—people who sought only to take rather than give in this moment of his suffering. Here, in the very hour, he was about to give everything he had for them, as he was on his death march, these people were here to suck whatever they could out of him. It was as if they had no compassion at all.

Jesus found himself in a state of deep despair. He had been able to keep himself focused on the faithful and his willingness to endure through all of this for them. But with the weight of the cross bearing down on his scarred back, with sweat and blood rolling off the thorns lodged in his skull and into his eyes, and with fatigue making his legs and insides quiver, his patience with the people was being tested.

Jesus cried out in frustration, "They come to touch me, to claim my power, yet they do not truly believe in it. He then thought, if they genuinely believed in me and the Father, I would not have to suffer through all of this.

All the pain, abuse, mockery, and exhaustion finally caught up with Jesus. He found his demeanor to sour, and his resolve was becoming questionable. As he thought about the events of the recent past . . . his arrest and the beating in the temple . . . the humiliation of being tied to a post and severely beaten . . . the crown of thorns he wore as he was mocked for being the Son of God . . . he suddenly became angry with the crowd. "Have I not suffered enough? Do they have to take from me what little strength I have left? Don't they care that I am doing all of this for them?" These were all thoughts that Jesus muttered to himself.

Jesus stopped to readjust the cross that pressed into his shoulder. He felt angry at the person who built this cross and his poor craftsmanship. "Why does it have to be so coarse?" he said aloud. The weight of the cross caused severe pain to his shoulders, and from time-to-time, Jesus would have to stop and switch the side on which he was carrying it. Jesus became incredibly angry at the cross he had to bear. He knew he had the authority to put it down and walk away at any time, and with that thought, his heart began to beat extremely fast. The sins of man inside of him seemed excited by the idea of Jesus walking away from his destiny.

The realization of the true foul nature of these sins almost defeated Jesus. Even when released from their originators and locked away in the most sacred of hearts, they took every opportunity to exploit man's shallowness. Jesus knew they called to his humanity. These sins were devoid of God. These burdens, these failings, were not his, nor did they belong to him. They were born of human frailty, a flaw that he knew all too well. In that moment, Jesus understood the truth—that within every heart, there was a part of man that would forever resist surrendering to God. It was from this place of defiance that sin was born.

Jesus understood the burden of the cross at that moment. The cross represented truth. The truth was that people were free to choose to be human and divine, just like Jesus. Jesus knew that people would never be able to fully give themselves to God. They were free to make that choice. Even the most beloved and holy of his followers would falter in faith and sin. If I wanted to, I could put the cross down and walk away, but I could never walk away from the truth, Jesus thought. The truth of man's weakness and lack of faith will be a burden I will carry for eternity. In that moment of clarity, Jesus understood that the true weight he bore was not the cross upon his shoulders nor the deep, searing pain from his wounds. It was the unshakable truth—the realization that humanity would never fully yield to the boundless grace of God. No matter the sacrifice, men would never love Him or the Father with the same depth, purity, and devotion with which they were loved.

These thoughts robbed Jesus of a great deal of motivation, but because of the threat of the whip, he kept moving along the path. His mind was a whirlwind of thoughts and emotions. The realization of the truth of man's weakness in faith seemed to become one with the cross. Not only was it heavy, but it was rough and grated against his very being. It caused Jesus pain—pain from which he could not escape. He felt all this and knew his pace had slowed considerably. Somewhere in the distance, he could hear the guards commanding him to keep going, to move faster. The noise of the crowd somehow blurred into a dull sound that seemed to resemble the stomping of a herd of sheep in the distance. He could hear the individual voices, but they were lost in everything else he was experiencing. His head spun, and he felt sick to his stomach. He knew what he was doing was the Father's will. He knew the Father allowed him to suffer out of his love for everyone, and Jesus knew this burden was necessary. But nonetheless, he still realized he was losing his motivation to continue.

Jesus wrestled with the thoughts that clouded his mind. His focus wavered, and for a brief moment, the weight of his purpose seemed distant. The thought that he could endure such agony, yet so many would still turn away from the truth, filled him with sorrow. In that fleeting moment, if it were not for the unwavering will of the Father, he might have laid down the cross and walked away, leaving the suffering behind. His spirit was defeated, and he was unaware that his pace had slowed even more. The crack of the guard's whip that rang in his ear brought Jesus out of his thoughts and back to the path. He gave the cross a heave to lift it so it could be repositioned on his shoulder, but then he became agonizingly aware of his shoulder pain. His feet felt like weights tied to his legs, and it took real effort to move them. Now that he was refocused back on the cross and his journey, he knew he had lost some of the will to charge up to Golgotha. He needed help. He lowered his head and looked back down at the path below him. His mind shifted to his Father in heaven, and he simply uttered the words "Please help me."

After a few more steps, he raised his head again to see, standing before him, was his mother. She was just a short distance away, and his pace quickened to reach her. He could see the darkness around her eyes, caused by lack of sleep, tears, and the pain of watching her son being tortured. He could tell she had been crying, but she was not now. He knew she would be strong for him because that was who she was. As he reached this wonderful woman whom he loved so much, Jesus stopped to let her reach out for him. At this, however, the guards grabbed Mary and tried to force Jesus to walk again, but the crowd pressed in on the two of them for their protection, insisting to the guards this was his mother. Upon hearing this, the guards reluctantly stepped back, granting Jesus and Mary a brief moment of solace. It seemed as though, in the depth of their hearts, they recognized the sacred bond between mother and son—one that transcended even the harshness of their duty. In that fleeting pause, they would not dare deny this woman the final embrace of her condemned child.

Mary grabbed Jesus and held him tightly, and Jesus closed his eyes, focusing on the warm, loving embrace. There is nothing like the love of one's mother. Mary was warm with her emotions and soft and gentle with her touch, but she also brought him strength through reassurance. It was such a wonderful and beautiful gift, one he desperately needed. Jesus took all of this in like a sponge. He didn't want to miss a single drop of the love Mary gave him. Her grace-filled embrace strengthened Jesus and gave him hope. He was humbled by his mother's charity. It seemed that, once again, she was willingly doing what God needed of her, even though it caused her much pain.

Jesus was filled with faith and love to the point of tears. "I do this for everyone, but I especially do it for you," he told his mother. His mother released him from her embrace to look at him. Jesus could see love and terror in her eyes at the same time. She reached for his face but hesitated to touch him. The crown of thorns made her gasp as she examined it. It was not how she wanted to see her handsome son, but Jesus looked at his mother and smiled. It was his desire to comfort her the way she had comforted him. Looking deep into her eyes and without saying a word, he let her know everything would be fine. Jesus calmed his mother, and she reached up and kissed him on the cheek. "I love you, my son," she said. Her kiss was the pinnacle of her beauty and grace, a tender symbol of her love. In all the moments they had shared, her kiss had always been a balm to his soul—this moment, too, was no different. Each time her lips met his cheek, a profound peace settled over him, as if the world's burdens lightened, if only for an instant.

The guards finally lost their patience with this reunion. One of them took Mary by the arm and escorted her off the path. For the sake of not causing more distress for her beloved Son, she willingly followed the man. She knew her moments spent with Jesus were a gift, but it was now over. She was aware that if she resisted, it would only cause confusion and possibly violence to break out. She knew that her son was as peaceful as he could be at this moment, and she did not want anything to disrupt that. Mary took all of this in, and she held it in her heart.

Jesus, happy to be renewed with a sense of purpose, didn't wait for the guards to prompt him to continue. Before a word was said, he lifted the cross again and began to walk. His soul was on fire, lit by the love only a mother can give. He was amazed at that moment that God had given such power to people. It was the power to move mountains, and that's what it felt like for Jesus. A mountain of hurt and pain had been lifted by his mother's love. His vision and purpose were clear once again. The sins of man and the hurt and cruelty they displayed had brought Jesus down and had brought him nothing but despair. But through Mary's beauty and grace, he felt alive again. His heart was filled with love and compassion for all.

She had reminded him how caring and generous people could be. She had reminded him how much people could love God and, therefore, how much they could love him. Reaching Golgotha had become more imperative than ever before. With a heart brimming with love and a renewed sense of hope for humanity, Jesus pressed forward.

With purpose and passion, Jesus forced his way along the path. His mind was filled with the desire to reach his goal. Focused thoughts of his mother, her beauty and grace, kept him moving. It also helped him forget some of the pain and his impending death. The joyous thought of Mary did wonders to lift his spirits, and this allowed his mind to wander away from his predicament and on to the people he loved. He thought of Peter and the other disciples. How much he had enjoyed the last three years of his life with them. The times they shared and the love that had grown into true fellowship warmed Jesus' heart. He reflected on Mary Magdalene, whom he cherished deeply, along with the other women who had faithfully served alongside them throughout his ministry. He took a moment to hold each of them in his heart. The awareness of their growth in God's Spirit, their transformation through love and faith, filled him with profound joy, offering a flicker of peace in the depths of his pain.

The glowing thoughts of his friends and mother served to warm his heart and lift his spirits. However, it could not change the fact that Jesus' legs were giving out on him. Even with a true resolve to reach his goal, he could not deny that his body seemed to be shutting down. The labor of placing one foot in front of the other while holding up the weight of the cross overwhelmed Jesus, and again, his pace slowed. The guards repeatedly shouted at Jesus to walk faster. He would attempt to comply, but any increase in speed would only last for a few steps, and then his legs would shake and seize up. The guards were frustrated with him, but they did not realize that it wasn't that Jesus didn't want to speed up—he simply couldn't. The guards became more hostile in their commands, but it did nothing to change his pace. Finally, one of the guards pulled out his whip and hit Jesus. The pain that ran through his body was immense. The lash of the whip seared his skin so badly that it felt like it was boiling. He closed his eyes and clenched his teeth in agony. Silently, he prayed to the Father, *Again, please help me.*

The guard lifted his whip to strike Jesus a second time when a voice screamed out from the crowd: "Stop!" The guard froze, his whip in midair. The command from the voice in the crowd seemed to have so much authority that everyone stopped what they were doing and stood there silently. An older man approached the guards. "Do you want this man to die before he even reaches the hilltop? Can't you see that death is upon him and he lacks the strength to make the journey? Do you beat a beast of burden to death when it is too tired and weakened to carry the load? No, you remove the load and send it to a dignified slaughter. Do the same for this man. If you want him to make it, you will have to help him."

Jesus understood this was the work of the Father. He could feel the presence of the Spirit around him. He knew it was the Spirit who had filled the man with compassion, boldness, and courage it took to confront the Roman guards and placed authority in his voice. The guard who was about to whip Jesus was still standing with the whip in the air. Everyone was looking at the guard, almost expecting him to help Jesus carry this cross himself. He lowered the whip slowly and looked around. He was not intending to help carry the cross; after all, he was a soldier in the Roman army. He would not subject himself to that kind of disgrace.

He continued to survey those surrounding Jesus, until he spotted, there on his left, a tall, strong-looking man at the back of the crowd. The guard, using his whip as a pointer, motioned toward the man and said, "You—you will help him." The man's face filled with shock and fear as he instinctively stepped back, his words stumbling over one another as he offered excuse after excuse for why he could not assist Jesus. His eyes darted to the guards, seeking an escape, hoping to distance himself enough to flee without drawing attention. But the guard's harsh command halted him in his tracks, and gripped by terror, he reluctantly obeyed. The guard, still pointing at the man with his whip, walked toward him. The people instantly part the way to avoid the whip, as if it were poisonous or cursed.

The guard walked over to this man and gave him a choice: "Either help this Jesus carry the cross or take his place." The young man, Simon, did not want to help Jesus. He did not want to walk through the streets looking like a condemned man. He was fearful that people would mistake him for the one to be crucified. But the guard pressed him for an answer. Simon did not reply. Then he looked into Jesus' eyes, and Jesus looked back at him. Jesus could see his fear and doubt—not only doubt in this situation but doubt in his own faith. Kindness and decency were also feelings Jesus received from him, mixed with overwhelming terror. Jesus prayed for the Spirit to fill this man, Simon, and remove his fear.

The guard approached Simon and was shouting at him at this point. He threatened to find Simon his own cross to carry and crucify him on it next to Jesus. For Simon, this had all become a blur. The sights and sounds around him seemed to slow down to a pace half their normal speed. He could hear the guard yelling and the noise of the crowd in the background. People were screaming and chanting, and the sound resonated in his ears like a chaotic mix of indecipherable noise. Simon kept his focus on Jesus. He was terrified of the way Jesus looked. The beatings had left him scarred, bruised, and bloody. His face was covered in dirt from the fall. The crown he wore on his head was ominous and appeared to be a symbol of evil. His clothes were covered in blood, and he was sweating profusely. He looked more like a street beggar than the promised Messiah. But even with Jesus' deplorable appearance, Simon could not look away from his soft and loving eyes. His gaze did not pierce defensively, but rather, it was inviting and welcoming. Without thought or a word, Simon began making his way toward Jesus. He seemed to have forgotten the fear that had gripped him originally. He hadn't even noticed it was absent. He walked to Jesus and took a longing look into his eyes, searching for something to make sense of the situation. And then he simply nodded his head and grabbed the cross, stepping underneath it and standing, raising the cross to his own height.

A flood of gratitude waved through Jesus, and he was filled with compassion for this man. This man had lifted the burden off his beaten and bruised shoulder, giving Jesus hope to see that even those who were unsure of their faith would still give in to the will of God. He was aware that Simon's heart was kind and filled with love. Jesus knew this man did not question God's existence, only his understanding of him. He knew it was the failure of the religious leaders that had made this man question his faith. Religion could not lead this man to salvation or *shalom*, peace with God on earth.

Jesus drew strength from Simon's unexpected assistance. As they carried the cross together toward Golgotha, he prayed that others would witness this simple act of compassion and kindness, seeing it as a reflection of the selfless love that God calls forth in all of us. The journey to God is not always without hardship, but those who answer His call to serve, no matter how difficult the task, will always find their way to Him.

There they were, the two of them, one man and one Messiah, walking side by side, sharing the burden of truth. As the two of them moved along on the path, there seemed to be more people than ever lining the streets. The cries and wails of the faithful seemed to fill the air. Jesus could still hear the laughter and jeers of those who did not believe, and it was okay. He would continue his mission for the salvation of all, especially for those who did not believe. Jesus looked at Simon as he quietly walked while carrying the lion's share of the weight of the cross. Jesus noticed that even with Simon's help, he was having trouble keeping his feet from stumbling. More than once along the way, Jesus lost the ability to lift his left leg high enough to push his foot forward. If it hadn't been for Simon's strength, they would both have lost their balance and fallen many times.

Jesus was fatigued to the point of exhaustion, yet his spirit was committed to the will of God, no matter the personal price for him. But however strong his spirit and faith were, he could not deny the weakness of his human body. His feet became heavier, and his legs grew stiff. His breathing came fast and shallow. His body needed air, but breathing deeply took an earnest effort and was accompanied by much pain, so short breaths would have to suffice. Jesus needed to rest, but he didn't request a break from the guards, for he knew it would be a waste of time. Instead, he became overheated. The weight of the cross strained his body, causing his fevered skin to burn with every step, but it was the weight of mankind's sins that tormented him most. With each agonizing moment, it felt as though an unquenchable fire blazed within him, intensifying with every stride. His mind became fixed on the heat of his body and the effort it took to walk. He needed a break—and the Father in heaven provided for his needs.

A beautiful woman, Veronica, slipped out of the crowd and blocked the path in front of them as she fell on her knees to honor Jesus. Her eyes were filled with tears, and Jesus could see the look of anguish on her face. He knew the weight she carried in her heart was for him. She loved him, and it was difficult for her to see him in so much pain. The woman's action took the guards by surprise. Before they really understood what was happening, she was there, in the middle of the path, on her knees in front of Jesus. She had nothing to offer him, but she desperately wanted to ease his pain any way she could. She lifted the rag she used to wipe her tears from her eyes and gave it to him. Jesus took the cloth and used it to wipe his own face. He was so thankful for this simple favor. His face was stiff with a combination of dirt and dried blood, and it was a relief to wipe it clean and clear his brows.

The brief encounter with Veronica left an indelible mark on Jesus' heart. As he wiped his face with the cloth she offered and returned it to her with a quiet gratitude, the guards seized her, pulling her away with harsh hands. She made no effort to resist, nor did she cry out in protest. Instead, she collapsed into their grasp, her body yielding not from defiance but from the weight of sorrow that had shattered her spirit. Jesus' state was more than she could bear to see. She believed in Jesus, and she remained faithful to him. After she was dragged back into the crowd, she began to weep—tears wrenching from the bottom of her soul. She could not contain her grief, and she wailed loudly for Jesus. She clutched the cloth he had used to wipe his face close to her heart and let her tears fall onto the ground.

Jesus' heart felt heavy for Veronica. Without command from the guard, Jesus and Simon both began walking again with the cross. This expediency was more Simon's doing than Jesus'. Jesus knew Simon was fearful of the guards and their quick willingness to use the whip. Jesus watched Veronica for the few steps it took to walk past her. He couldn't hear anything else, but the wails and screams of this distraught woman, and his heart broke for her. They continued along the path, and for the next few moments, Jesus could think of nothing but his brief encounter with the woman with such a big heart. It moved him so greatly that his eyes welled up with tears.

He was so thankful that Veronica had presented him with a cloth to wipe his face. And he was also extremely thankful that her distraction had allowed him the opportunity to rest, even for a moment. His leg muscles had been fatigued to the point of seizing, and the brief break was all that was needed to relax so they could work again. Jesus knew it was the Holy Spirit who had prompted Veronica to lend assistance and allowed her to slip past the guards. Jesus thanked God for providing for him in his time of need.

Jesus struggled to block out the crowd that lined the path before him. Each face, filled with curiosity, disdain, or indifference, weighed heavily on his heart. Every glance from them seemed to add more weight to his already burdened steps. Yet, with every ounce of will, he forced himself to look away, knowing that if he was to reach the end of this suffering, he could not afford to be distracted by their gazes, no matter how piercing.

He lowered his gaze to the ground. It was easier this way. He kept his focus on the path ahead and concentrated on moving. He didn't have to pay attention to where he was heading. All he had to do was follow Simon's lead. He kept his head down and pushed on, thinking about nothing but the next step. As time passed, exhaustion finally caught up with him again. It appeared that no matter how firm his resolve was to carry out the will of the Father, he could not overcome the frailty of his body. His body, already battered by unimaginable torment, began to betray him. A sharp, stabbing pain pierced his abdomen, its source elusive yet undeniable. It was not the specific location that troubled him but the relentless discomfort that clouded his mind. The agony surged through him, clouding his thoughts and draining what little focus he had left. His skin, no longer glistening with sweat, trembled in response to the chill creeping over him. Every movement became an effort, and a wave of nausea churned within him, threatening to overwhelm him completely. He could taste nothing but acid in his mouth, and his eyes lost focus. The path ahead of him blurred all at once. But Jesus was determined to continue, so he grabbed the cross with a new hold. He used what remaining strength he had left and pushed harder with each leg to keep himself moving forward. This renewed resolve did not make things better. The path in front of him blurred even more, and his eyes started darting back and forth in rapid succession. He closed them to refocus, but it was no use. Jesus felt himself slipping from consciousness. He tried to stop it from happening, but it was to no avail; he was passing out. The world became black, and he felt his knees buckle. He let go of the cross and collapsed onto the ground.

For Jesus, time seemed to stretch painfully, each moment heavy with suffering. But for Simon, the passage of time was a blur. Lost in the effort to carry the weight of the cross, Simon had been so absorbed in the path ahead that he hadn't noticed the sudden shift. One moment, the burden was shared, and the next, it was entirely his own. As Jesus collapsed, Simon's grip faltered, and the weight of the cross overwhelmed him. He tried to steady it, but the ground rushed up beneath him, and with a sickening thud, he and the cross fell together.

Simon grabbed the cross and held it, and as he fell, he guided the cross to the ground to protect Jesus and himself from its weight. Despite Simon's best efforts, the cross crashed down with a brutal force, pinning both him and Jesus to the ground. The weight of the heavy beams crushed down on Simon, and he gasped under the immense pressure. Instinctively, he gripped the cross with trembling hands, trying desperately to lift it off them both. The pain from the fall and the impact of the cross was sharp and unrelenting. As Simon struggled, he couldn't help but imagine the agony Jesus must have felt, trapped beneath the weight, already battered and broken. The thought of enduring such pain while carrying such a burden stirred deep sympathy and awe in Simon's heart.

Many people in the crowd pressed in to lend assistance, and the guards, fearful of the mob, began yelling and shouting. They brought out their whips and swords to beat the people back away from them and Jesus. Simon picked himself up from the ground then lifted the cross. As Simon gazed down at Jesus' lifeless form, a pang of dread seized his chest. He feared Jesus might never rise again. A cold, paralyzing thought struck him like a bolt of lightning: What if Jesus couldn't get up? Would the guards force him to bear the cross in Jesus' stead? The weight of this possibility filled Simon with a wave of terror, and a vivid, haunting vision flashed before his eyes—of himself, bound and condemned, nailed to the cross in place of Jesus. The terror of being mistaken for a condemned man flooded his thoughts, but just as despair began to take hold, a flicker of movement stirred in Jesus' body. He looked back at Jesus' prone body, but to his utter relief, he finally saw movement.

As Jesus lay on the ground, he tried to piece the last few moments back together in his mind. He knew he had been carrying the cross, and he remembered his knees growing weak. Now, he found himself lying on the ground in pain. Through the fog in his brain, he remembered falling and hearing the screams from the crowd. He realized that he had passed out for a few moments, or at least he thought it was a few moments. Jesus' eyes, heavy with exhaustion, scanned the chaos as the guards pushed the crowd back. Simon's voice cut through the fog, urging him to rise. For a moment, pain threatened to keep him down, but with quiet strength, Jesus gathered his resolve. He cleared his mind, the fog lifting just enough to push through the exhaustion. With a labored breath, he lifted his chest off the ground and slowly rose. His rising brought sighs of relief from the crowd, and Simon felt more at ease. Jesus was still unsteady, but that didn't stop him from approaching the cross. He positioned himself beneath it and once again lifted the burden of its weight. Simon, much more concerned about Jesus than himself at this point, asked if he was all right to continue. Jesus just gave a quick nod and motioned to Simon to proceed.

Without hesitation, Simon followed Jesus' command and continued down the path. Jesus did not speak at all. He knew his strength was fleeting and would not last. He wanted more than anything to rest, but he feared that if they stopped, he would not be able to start again. It was imperative to him that everyone understood this was his task that this was his cross to bear. He knew these moments would hold lasting significance, destined to inspire countless souls across time.

He understood that his endurance would set a sacred standard, inspiring those called to suffer for their faith to persevere. His faithfulness, even unto death, was the ultimate devotion that God deserved. Not only that, if he failed, what would become of mankind's sins? He could not leave them here on this path. He had a destination for them. There was a price to be paid, and he would pay it—for nothing less would secure man's salvation. The weight of mankind's salvation filled his mind completely. Failure was not an option, for if he faltered, humanity would be lost. He could not permit the frailties of his human form to be the cause of that failure. He wished at that moment that his human frame had the same resolve and strength as his faith. However, the fragility of his structure was more than ever on his mind.

Jesus glanced over to look at his companion, Simon. He could tell that this journey was taking its toll. Simon was sweating heavily, and his breathing had become deep and rapid. Jesus was thankful this man had been willing to help. He knew he could not have completed the mission without him. Simon's pace had slowed with the distance they traveled, and Jesus was thankful for this. Still, though he was glad the pace had slowed, it also worried him. He was not sure if his body could hang on long enough to reach the top of the hill—but regardless, he pressed on.

Given Jesus' tired and weakened state, merely walking would have been a challenge, but the added weight of the cross made the task almost impossible. His body was shutting down, and there was nothing he could do to stop it. The searing pain in his stomach surged back, sharper and deeper than before. Jesus sensed an internal anguish beyond what he could bear, yet he also knew that worrying for himself was no longer relevant. That time had passed. With resolute focus, he set his mind on the hill before him, knowing he must ascend. But as the incline grew steeper, every step demanded a height and power that his weary legs almost could not deliver. Still, his determination to fulfill this journey surpassed the fading strength in his body, driving him forward, step by grueling step.

Jesus was now straining beyond the limits he had ever imagined, each step along the path feeling like an eternity. His breath came in shallow, desperate gasps, and no matter how deeply he tried to draw in air, it seemed his lungs could not fill enough to sustain his body's demands. Each gasp fell short, and he felt himself slipping further into a void of exhaustion. With each step, he also found the pain in his abdomen strengthening, now joined by an additional pain in his chest. He found it impossible to focus on anything but the misery of the situation. Exhaustion and pain fogged his mind while his body shook from head to toe. He could no longer focus on anything, nor could he even picture anything or anyone. He was unsure what was keeping him moving. He was even lost as to where he was in the world. His mind became blank, and he felt as if he was floating.

The harsh truth was that he wasn't floating; he was plummeting. For the third time, Jesus' body gave way, and he fell to the ground with a force that defied his will. This time, he was entirely unaware as he sank into unconsciousness, his body crumbling to the earth beneath the weight of his burden. Simon also was unaware of the extent to which Jesus was struggling. He had not been paying attention to him at all. He had simply been focused on getting up the hill and to the end of this journey. So, when Jesus collapsed, Simon was caught off guard. This time, Simon was unable to do anything to steer the cross away from him and Jesus, and he and the cross fell together. The full weight of the cross landed on Jesus and Simon with it. Once more, Simon, driven by both panic and urgency, scrambled to his feet, his heart pounding as he steadied himself. A wave of relief washed over him as he caught sight of Jesus, still struggling beneath the cross. Yet, a deepening fear gripped him—the dread that Jesus, weakened and suffering, might not survive the grueling path ahead.

Once Jesus realized he had fallen once again, he could hear the laughter, screams, and cries, and he opened his eyes. He blinked wildly for a moment, waiting for the world to come back into focus. As things became clearer, he could make out a myriad of faces where he expected to see feet. It was as though everyone had hit the ground when he did to, try to see if he was still alive. The fear and desperation he observed in their eyes motivated him to try to rise again to his feet. He hated to see the pain on their faces. This time, however, the fall had a much more significant impact. The blow from the cross, combined with Simon's weight on top of it, had taken his air away. As his mind became more focused, he discovered he was gasping for breath. He also realized his insides hurt much more than they had before the fall. Some kind of internal damage must have happened as a result. The pain within him intensified, reaching an unbearable crescendo. Every torment he bore—the thorns piercing his scalp, the raw wounds across his back, the bruises from relentless beatings, and the unrelenting ache in his abdomen—now coalesced with a new, searing pain deep within his chest. His entire being throbbed in agony, not a single place on his body untouched by suffering. Though his spirit whispered courage to rise and press on, his frail, exhausted body pleaded for stillness, craving only an end to this torrent of anguish.

Jesus felt the relief of Simon removing the cross off his body. It was as if the weight of the world had been lifted from his soul. He did not understand how, but the weight of the cross had bound him to the earth.

Jesus gave thanks to the Father in heaven and tried to ignore the pain, ignore the exhaustion, and ignore the blood pooling on the ground. He shut out the taunts and scorn that surrounded him, dismissing every feeling that rose within him but one. He anchored himself to that solitary, unwavering emotion: love.

He thought of the beautiful souls he had encountered: Moses, Elijah, John the Baptist, Peter, and others. He brought to mind the many women who had served him in his ministry, especially Mary Magdalene, his blessed mother, and the multitude of others who would come after his death. These beautiful images brought peace to his spirit and calmed his wild thoughts. He placed Abba and all of creation in the center of his mind's eye. He marveled in awe when he pictured the setting sun and the way the moon and the stars lit up the night sky. He could see the face of God in all of it.

The Father would have known how difficult this journey would be, so he gave it to the only one he could trust, His beloved Son. Jesus knew it broke the Father's heart to see him suffer so terribly, but for the love of his creation, it had to be done. Jesus allowed emotion of overwhelming love to fill his body to the brink of overflowing. He was close now. All he had to do was walk up this hill, and he would have made it to the location where he would be glorified. The end was in sight, and triumph was near, resonating in his heart like a distant hymn. He knew he could not stop now—every fiber of his being was fixed upon reaching that sacred summit.

Once again, with a renewed sense of purpose, Jesus repositioned his hands to lift his upper body off the ground. Without thinking about the pain, he forced his torso up, clumsily folded his legs under his upper body, and tried to stand. This task would have been much more difficult if it hadn't been for one of the guards grabbing Jesus by the arm and helping to pull him to his feet. As Jesus stood upright, he let out a loud moan of agony. He didn't appreciate the haste with which the guard had used to get him up, but he was thankful for the assistance. Jesus looked up at the hill in front of him. He didn't have far to go now, but it was all uphill from here. He turned to look at Simon. Simon's eyes were still full of fear and doubt. Jesus knew Simon was afraid that Jesus would not be able to finish the climb up the hill. He saw doubt on Simon's face, and so he gave him a small but reassuring smile. Then he limped over to the cross and took his place alongside Simon. Together, they took up the weight of the cross and started their ascent up the hill.

The climb was slow and difficult for Jesus, and Simon was doing all he could at this point to carry the bulk of the weight. He watched Jesus intently with every step they took. Simon, fearful that Jesus might collapse once more, stayed vigilant, prepared to throw the cross aside before it could come crashing down upon them both. His heart raced with the tension of every faltering step, ready to act at a moment's notice to shield Jesus from further harm. Amazingly, Jesus kept pace. He breathed harder than ever, and Jesus could feel his heart beating hard as it pulsed wildly in his head. He walked with his eyes closed, but this time, he was not taking the lead from Simon. There was something else guiding Jesus up the hill. The Holy Spirit was present with Jesus, guiding each step and freeing his mind to drift inward. Sheltered by this divine presence, Jesus found solace in his thoughts, momentarily distant from the pain and turmoil surrounding him. He did not have to focus on the path, the weight, the pain, the sorrow, or the grief. He had given himself completely to the Holy Spirit, and the Spirit moved Jesus along blindly. Jesus was unsure how long the trip up the hill lasted, but before he realized it, it was over.

*"Do not judge me by my successes, judge me by how many times
I fell down and got back up again."*

—Nelson Mandela

CHAPTER 5

The Crucifixion

❖ ● ❖

As Jesus and Simon ascended the final stretch and reached the summit, a command was given for them to halt. In unison, they released their grip, allowing the weight of the cross to drop heavily to the ground, the burden lifted from their shoulders, if only for a fleeting moment. The effort to carefully place it on the ground was more than either of them wanted to expend, so they simply let it fall. Simon was particularly relieved to be free of this symbol of death. He looked around and noticed that no one was paying attention to him at this point. Lingering fear still gnawed at him, a worry that he might be mistaken for a condemned man himself. With a final, conflicted glance, he took a step back, cautiously distancing himself from the scene, retreating from the weight of what he had just shared. He hadn't taken many steps before something made him freeze. Jesus had collapsed on the ground again. Immediately, Simon's fear left him as his concern for Jesus filled his heart. For some reason, he felt a new bond with this man.

Jesus remained a haunting sight, his face marred by blood and bruises, embodying the raw suffering etched into his very being. His clothes were filthy and covered in blood. His face was once again covered in dirt, and the crown of thorns screamed out as a threatening sign. It was without explanation, but to Simon, Jesus' appearance contradicted what he believed a man should look like, no matter the circumstances. He looked offensive and obscene, like a wild dog that had been caught in a thicket of thorns. But the difference was his face. It appeared soft and warm, like the dawn on a clear summer morning. His eyes held an intensity that Simon had never encountered, as if they contained an ocean's depth and a sky's endless reach. Looking into them felt like gazing into the universe itself—profound, boundless, and filled with mysteries untold. It was a glance that held every sorrow, every hope as if the stars themselves resided within that silent, unyielding gaze. He was filled with wonder and awe—as well as questions. It came to him at that moment that he had not even wondered why Jesus was being crucified. He knew that somehow Jesus had opposed the Jewish leaders, but he did not understand the actual crime. Simon had simply taken it for granted, at the beginning of this journey, that Jesus was a guilty man. But guilty of what? he wondered. Why would a condemned man push himself so hard to climb that hill? He could have just continued to lie on the ground where he had fallen the first time. That would have forced the guards to arrange for him to be carried the rest of the way. It became painfully apparent to Simon that Jesus felt it was important to carry the cross himself.

Simon couldn't fathom the depth of Jesus' purpose or the unwavering resolve that carried him forward. In that moment, he recognized that every assumption he'd made about this man was misguided. He looked again into Jesus' eyes and found a calm sea of compassion. There was nothing cold or harsh about Jesus' gaze. In fact, it was the opposite. Simon could see love and life in his eyes. He found something that made him feel warm on the inside and good about himself. This was not a man who deserved death. In a place of such harshness and suffering, Jesus' presence felt strangely out of place, as if his gaze alone brought a calm that was foreign to this hill—or perhaps, Simon thought, it was simply the peace he himself felt unexpectedly in Jesus' presence.

Simon had been worried about what would happen when they reached the top of the hill, and the events turned out to be unexpected. He had backed away from Jesus and the cross so easily, but now that he was separated from them, he wanted to be closer. In an inexplicable way, walking this path beside Jesus had forged a bond deeper than Simon could have foreseen; through shared suffering and unspoken understanding, Jesus had become like a brother to him. Here, at the end, at Golgotha, he wanted to know this man—he wanted to hear what Jesus had to say. They had not spoken to each other while they were carrying the cross. Simon wished he had taken the opportunity to learn who Jesus was when he'd had the chance. The sadness he felt for Jesus found companionship with the sadness he felt for himself. Simon felt a pang of sorrow as he realized he might always carry an unanswered question about who this man truly was. A quiet regret settled in his heart, knowing he would never fully understand the mystery and depth of Jesus.

Jesus and Simon still looked at each other for several moments after the cross was dropped to the ground. Simon suspected Jesus knew exactly what he was thinking. And Jesus, so thankful that Simon had been there to help him, brought peace to Simon, quieting the questions that were running through his mind. Simon was unsure how, but he knew Jesus was grateful for his help. Feeling satisfied that the events of the day had been orchestrated by design rather than occurring by some cruel, random act of violence, Simon once again began backing away from the scene. Jesus gave him a final nod of acceptance, which Simon returned. And with that, Simon walked back down the hill. He did not look back. He left with the sense that he had done something good, even though he did not understand what or why. A sense of fulfillment washed over him as he felt that his efforts had not only eased Jesus' burden but had woven a bond between them. Simon knew he had earned the friendship of someone extraordinary.

As Simon moved down the hill, Jesus turned to see what was happening around him. The crowds of people who had lined the path leading to this place were now gathering in the area. The guards and soldiers patrolled, keeping the crowds at bay. They made sure the area was not overrun by the gathering hordes. Once the guards had firmly established lines for the people to view the spectacle, they turned their attention to Jesus. The soldiers showed no urgency to proceed with the crucifixion. Instead, they lingered, gathering in a loose circle and launching into a discussion peppered with bursts of laughter, their voices echoing with unsettling ease amidst the gravity of the moment. Jesus saw how the guards kept glancing over at him as they spoke, and he wished this whole thing was over. He found himself frustrated with everything. He had pushed himself beyond the point of exhaustion, beyond his tolerance for pain. He did not want any more delays, and he especially did not want to endure whatever was being schemed up by the guards.

The wait to find out the purpose of the discussion among the guards and soldiers was short. Two guards soon approached Jesus and lifted him to his feet. With quick and violent movements, they stripped his clothes from his body. The movements themselves were painful, but they paled next to the ripping open of almost every wound on his body. Experiencing this torture when he had been given the crown of thorns was horrible enough. This repeated performance was not welcome, and this time was no less painful than the others. The difference was that this time, his scars were in view for everyone to look at. What brought it to everyone's attention were Jesus' moans of agony as he was stripped. Many of the women, seeing Jesus' scarred and bleeding body, began to cry and openly wailed for him. They gazed upon his wounded form, stunned by the depths of his pain, and couldn't help but wonder how he bore such agony and disgrace with an unshaken dignity, even as he walked toward death.

The soldiers grabbed the cross and placed it on the ground where Jesus was to be crucified. Afterward, they walked back over to get Jesus. They proceeded as a group, expecting him to put up some resistance, but there was none. Jesus was anxious to be on his cross. He did not wish to die, but he knew that when his flesh died, he would be fully alive in the Spirit. Jesus had enjoyed his time on the earth, but he was eager to return to the Father. To the astonishment of the guards, Jesus took the lead, moving from where he stood toward the place where the cross awaited him. With quiet resolve, he walked ahead, his steps steady, as though he were guiding himself toward his own fate. He knew what to do: He lay down on the cross and prepared for one last bout with excruciating pain.

Jesus tried to steady himself on the narrow cross, but he could not. He was simply too weak. Guards kneeled on either side of him and tied his arms to the cross to hold his body still. His right arm was grabbed and held straight out from his side. He looked over in time to see the first of the spikes rest its point on his hand. The person who was going to nail Jesus to this cross was skilled at the task. He knew exactly where to place the nail, and without hesitation, he hit it with a large hammer, driving it through Jesus' hand and into the wooden cross. A pain beyond all that Jesus had experienced up to now ran through him, causing him to slam his head back against the cross and driving the thorny crown even deeper into his skull. Jesus felt like his arm bones had been replaced by hot irons, and something stabbed him in the right eye. He felt a wave of pain run through his entire body, but before he could take another breath, the nail was hit for the second time. This hurt as much as the first strike. His neck had become stiff, and his head pounded with pain. He felt his heartbeat as if it were desperately trying to escape his chest, and he imagined the only thing keeping it there was the heavy weight of the sins of man, which were pressing so hard on him that he struggled to breathe. Jesus' hands shook uncontrollably, and his stomach roiled while a surge of heat burst through his head. The pain that surged through his body surpassed anything he could have ever conceived, each heartbeat echoing with an intensity that seemed almost unendurable as if his very essence was being tested beyond its limits.

After a few more strikes against the nail, the guard stood to his feet, crossed to the other side, and began work on the other hand. Jesus' mind was on fire with the pain and emotion at this point. His head felt like something was growing inside it that would split his skull open. The skilled executioner wasted no time driving the spike into Jesus' other hand. Jesus could endure the pain, but not without screaming out in agony. In this moment, he felt the tug of his human nature surge within him, a deep-rooted urge to flee or strike back against the cruelty surrounding him. The part of him bound to earthly instincts fought fiercely, urging him to escape this agony or retaliate against these men who seemed so lost in malice. Jesus knew he had the power to release himself from this torture, to instantly heal his wounds. There was something alive in the fibers of this human body that wanted the pain to end, and it was willing to do anything to accomplish that. When the nails had finally pierced his feet, for a split second, Jesus thought he might lose consciousness due to the pain. His breaths came rapid and shallow, yet they seemed powerless to relieve the suffocating strain within him. Each gasp felt hollow, a futile attempt to draw in air that seemed just out of reach. He pushed himself to inhale harder, feeling as if the very life he clung to was slipping away, his body craving oxygen with a desperation that defied all he had known. With every labored breath, he tried to inhale as deeply as possible. However, the pain in his core limited the amount of air he could pull into his lungs. Jesus needed something to focus on to take his mind off the pain. He searched for any thought to distract himself, reaching for memories, hopes, even prayers—but the ache in his heart eclipsed them all, consuming his mind with a sorrow too deep to escape.

His heart was beating so fast that Jesus could feel his pulse in every cell of his body. There was not a spot on his body that was not throbbing with pain. A surge of anger rose within him, unexpected and difficult to contain. Jesus wrestled with his own thoughts, bewildered by the intensity of his frustration. Where was the peace he had always known from the Father and the Holy Spirit? Why did his heart pound so fiercely, and why did the pain seem so relentless, refusing his will to subdue it? He suffered through the torture of having his feet nailed to the cross, unable to take his mind off the pain. He finally gave in and focused on the one thing he could not escape: his pounding heart. Jesus turned his focus to the heart within him—a vessel created to hold boundless love—and sought to understand why it now felt shrouded in darkness. As he looked deeply inward, a profound realization settled over him. The immense suffering he bore was woven into the sins of mankind, each one a weight pressing down on his spirit.

Many of the sins Jesus carried in his heart were the result of actions taken by people who were in deep pain. When he looked beyond the sins, he saw the pain of the people who had committed them, and Jesus understood why his body cried out for release from this torture. Countless sins had been born from humanity's instinct to flee from pain, to evade the hardship of their reality. In his heart, Jesus felt a profound sorrow for them—a sorrow deeper than the physical anguish he endured. His tears were not for his own suffering but for the faith they lacked, for their unwillingness to trust in the strength and love of the Father.

Jesus consoled himself as he calmed his thoughts and suppressed the negative emotions. He allowed his love for all to fill every space of his being, especially his heart. After feeling the pain of so many people, he wrapped his heart in a shield of golden love. This gave it a glorious case in which to deliver the sins of mankind to the Father. And with that, he made a vow that no one would ever have to suffer through any such pain without him again. For every sorrow, he would be there to share it, to shoulder the weight of their burdens, and to offer comfort in the stillness of the heart. He resolved to hold an open invitation to forgive, especially for those sins born from suffering, promising that no agony would go unseen and that his love would be a sanctuary for those seeking refuge. He would become known as the Prince of Peace. He would bring peace to those suffering from pain.

As his mind returned to what was happening, he saw that one of the guards carried a sign which said, THE KING OF THE JEWS. The guard lifted the sign high for his fellow soldiers to see, igniting another round of mocking laughter. In their jeering faces, Jesus felt the sting of scorn meant to belittle and wound. The guards laughed and snickered as the sign was nailed to the cross above Jesus' head. After the sign was mounted, the guards stood back and admired their work. After a few more jokes and laughs, they then returned to their assigned tasks. They grabbed Jesus and the cross and raised them both upright. Jesus thought the pain he had been in while lying on the ground would have been the most awful of all. Yet even this paled in comparison to the agony that coursed through him as his body's weight pressed down upon the nails once the cross stood upright. Each heartbeat intensified the searing pain radiating through his limbs. Jesus found himself vertical and in agony. It seemed that every time he got used to one source of pain, he was exposed to yet another. His arms pulled on their sockets intensely. He could feel the flesh in his hands rip slightly as they adjusted to supporting his body weight. Again, he was in pain to the point of passing out. His breaths came in labored gasps as he fought to steady himself, willing his mind to stay clear, to resist the pull of unconsciousness. Every inhale was a battle, a fierce struggle to remain present in this final act of sacrifice. He could feel his upper lip and nose go numb. He knew he would pass out soon if he could not get the pain under control. He needed something to focus on to distract him. He tried looking down at the people in the crowd to see if something could take his mind off his position. He found what he wanted, but it was an incredibly sad scene.

The guards had picked up his clothes and begun to cast lots. Jesus now understood what the discussion had all been about before he was nailed to the cross. As the guards placed his garments up for bid, Jesus was appalled at the number of people trying to buy them. Some wanted a souvenir to try to sell later for profit. Others wanted any piece of Jesus they could get. They simply desired a prize to keep in their house. This was as if the fabric that touched the Messiah would provide them with favor or good fortune. Isn't it amazing how lost these souls are? Jesus thought.

With every step of this process, Jesus became increasingly aware that without him and this sacrifice, love would be lost on these people. He should have felt angry that they were making a game out of his life. He should have been furious that some people were trying to profit from his death, but he was not. Instead, he was filled with compassion and love. In some strange way, it was okay for them to profit from him. After all, wasn't that why he was here? Wouldn't all people benefit from him hanging on the cross? He found what they were doing to be in poor taste, but the irony of the entire situation seemed almost fitting.

Seeing the guards cast lots for his clothes distracted Jesus while his body adjusted to this new situation. The pain was still immense, but he was coming to terms with it. Jesus was now calm enough to examine the people who had gathered in front of the cross and focus on who they were. He looked around and saw so many of his loved ones. He tried to pick out as many of them as possible, but his neck was beginning to tire. In fact, it was more than his neck that was feeling the effects of fatigue. He was exhausted to the core of his being. Jesus wasn't sure if it was his fatigued neck muscles that made it challenging to keep his head up or if it was that he was just so exhausted that he lacked the will to do it. Given what he had been through in the last few hours, it was difficult to tell. Jesus was uncertain what his body even felt like anymore. He had been pushed to the very limits of what a human body could endure. He realized at that moment that certain parts of his body seemed to have no feeling at all. The pain he felt in his chest did not hurt as much. It now felt like something was swelling up inside him, taking up more room than it should. It was a feeling he had never experienced before, and he really didn't know what it meant. He knew that whatever was happening inside of his body was horrible, but he could see no reason to worry. He was at the end of his life here on earth, and now, more than ever, it was time to be centered on the spirit, not the body. His body would fail shortly, and he would move on to be with the Father.

Jesus reflected on his life mission here on the earth. Once again, the warm thoughts of his mother filled his soul. It was a pleasure, at least in his mind, to hear her soft voice and feel her gentle and loving touch. The thought of the grief this was causing her was almost more than Jesus could bear. With immense effort, he pushed against his feet, lifting his bruised and weary body just enough to draw a fuller breath. Each movement ignited sharp agony throughout his limbs, yet this painful ascent was the sole means to fill his lungs with the air he desperately needed. As he exhaled, he forced himself to lift his neck and search for his mother. As expected, she wasn't far away, so finding her wasn't difficult. When he looked at her, instantly, his heart was filled with sympathy and love. It was complete and broken at the same time. He could not leave this beautiful and wonderful woman to fend for herself. It was his responsibility to care for her as she aged, but because of the Father's mission, he could not do so. This distressed him greatly, and he found himself filled with grief again. He needed to ensure she would be provided for throughout the remainder of her days.

Standing by the cross of Jesus were his mother and his mother's sister, Mary wife of Clopas, and Mary of Magdala. When Jesus saw his mother and the disciple there whom he loved, he said to his mother, "Woman, behold, your son." Then he said to the disciple, "Behold, your mother." And from that hour the disciple took her into his home.

—John 19:25–27

It brought comfort to Jesus to be assured that Mary would be well cared for. She had been entrusted to one of his own. Jesus felt a profound peace, knowing that John's heart overflowed with genuine love and devotion. He entrusted his mother to a soul as caring as his own, someone who would guard her with the same reverence and compassion she had shown him throughout his life. He found solace in the certainty that, though he would watch over her from heaven, Mary would be sheltered by hands and a heart he could trust completely. Until her time came to join him in glory, she would be cherished and protected.

The relief of knowing his mother would be cared for lessened Jesus' burden, and he found himself much more at ease. He was still writhing in pain and could no longer focus on what was in front of him. His skin was hot from the sun, and his mouth was dry to the point he found it difficult to speak. Betrothing his mother to his beloved brother had made him aware of how painful speaking was. His throat was parched and tight, and the words came through like hot coals, burning and scraping as they passed from his throat to his lips. He decided to conserve his strength by not speaking if he didn't have to. However, there was so much he desperately wanted to say at this moment. He desired to console those who felt grief because of his situation. He wished he could explain why he was hanging on the cross. He recognized that many people thought he was crazy, and many thought he was nothing more than a false prophet. He wanted to proclaim the glory of God here on the cross, but his body did not have the strength. It seemed he lacked the will to use this moment to assist those who believed in him and teach them what it meant. He knew they sought after this, but they would have to wait for their faith to show them the wisdom of the day.

Jesus heard the voices from the crowd calling to him. There were those who mocked him. They yelled out to him that if he was really the Messiah, he should save himself, and then they would believe. Ending his time on the cross was a welcome thought, but he knew the mission was not yet complete. He wondered if anyone recognized that he deeply held the authority to come down from the cross. He could heal his wounds and proclaim God's glory right here on the spot. He knew that if he did that very thing, so many knees would bend to worship him—but out of fear. Didn't they realize the purpose of his life was to bring a message of love and show them how to triumph over fear? The Jews feared God, and they taught all to fear God. "Fear of God's wrath is wise, but you cannot reach God through fear," Jesus said to himself. "Why is this so difficult for them to understand?" Jesus knew he could command the sky to open and have a legion of angels come to his aid. However, by doing so, he would be undoing his life's work. He would have lost all he had gained for the Father. Jesus had come to plant the seeds of love. It was time for man to stop placing fear in front of their faith and replace that fear with faith, love, and good works with the word charity.

Jesus turned his heart away from the voices taunting him to save himself, aware that in time, the world would understand the depth of these harrowing moments. What appeared as despair and defeat would be seen for what it truly was—the most profound act of love and self-sacrifice. He knew his suffering would reveal a love vast enough to encompass everyone, a love that transcended even death. He willingly did it for both the righteous and the lost sheep. The fact was, he did this more for those with little or no faith than for those with great faith. How many times had he said it: "A healthy man does not need a doctor." Jesus came to save the sinners, the very people who had heckled and mocked him. For now, it was enough. In time, the world would come to understand the necessity of this sacrifice, the profound purpose behind each painful step. Jesus closed his eyes to block out the surrounding sights and sounds. He wanted a brief escape from the mockery and the cries and moans of the faithful. He was tired to the point of death. The events of the day, combined with a lack of sleep, had left him weakened, but this feeling ran deeper than that. He was tired from the entirety of his mission. Day after day, he had reached out to people to explain the will of God. And so much of what he said was ignored. It was not that this surprised him, but it was enough to wear him down. At times, he felt the actual sheep in the field would have understood and come to believe faster than these people. They just could not give up the ways of the flesh and live in the Spirit. Jesus knew he had planted the seeds of faith again. It seemed ironic to him how many times this seed had been planted. He thought about it, and ironic wasn't really the word to describe the phenomenon. The word that most accurately described the situation was sad. Jesus didn't want to use that word out of love for his children, but it was true.

God had planted the seed with Adam, and he had forsaken God by eating the forbidden fruit. God then destroyed the earth and replanted it with Noah, and man still refused to yield to his will. This forced God to create a new beginning with Abraham and reinforce his will through Moses. He led his people out of captivity and saved them from death, only to have them reject his love. It seemed that no matter what God did, man chose death over life every time. They would claim to love and honor him, but when it came time to put their words into action, they fell short. Did these people not realize the reason God sent his only Son was to plant the seed of love again, a love that would lead them to salvation? It was terrible enough that these people had a long history of rejecting their Creator, but now they had hung his son on a cross. A death suited for the most deplorable of criminals was now deemed fitting for the one who was sent to save them. Jesus could feel the rejection the Father felt and was deeply saddened.

Jesus marveled at human consistency. He thought about how their lack of faith led to history repeating itself. Because this generation of people was so lost, they reminded him of the Israelites wandering in the desert. This was when the Jews were in Rephidim, and there was no water to drink. He remembered how hostile they had become to Moses, demanding he give them fresh water. These people had not changed at all. Jesus remembered meeting the woman at the well when he had asked her for a drink. Once Jesus told her of the life-giving water, she, too, demanded it. It had been many generations between the two instances, and yet the issue was still the same. It was not the absence of water that left them parched but the absence of faith. So, Moses, under God's command, had struck the rock, and a river had flowed for them to drink. Jesus struck his rock, Peter. From Peter, a river of faith would flow to build a new church. Jesus warmly thought of Peter; even with all his faults, there was no one better for this task. Peter drank deeply from the cup of faith, and who better to lead the church than the one who filled himself completely with the Spirit?

Jesus was lost in thought about how things had not really changed for this group of people since their forty years of wandering in the desert. God had provided for them in their exile by giving them manna, bread from heaven, to eat. These nomadic people were hungry, and in the barren desert, God offered them food. Jesus, recognizing the people were still hungry for God and his glory, gave himself as the Bread of Life. Once again, God provided for their needs from heaven. He gave me time to nourish them, Jesus thought. His life, deeds, teachings, and body would be the new bread of the covenant, bread that would feed their souls for eternity. Jesus wondered how long it would take the people to realize this. He would feed them as they needed. All they had to do was ask.

Jesus thought about his purpose for coming to the earth. Many will say that I came to die, but that is not so. I came so they could live. One must die in the flesh to find life, Jesus thought. He prayed that many would follow his example and choose to live in God's grace. He pondered whether they would come to understand that just as Moses had delivered them from the chains of earthly toil into the promise of a land flowing with milk and honey, he was here to deliver them from the bondage of sin into the boundless freedom of everlasting salvation.

In an instant, Jesus' mind drifted back to the past, and he found himself struck by the undeniable parallels between this crowd and their ancestors who had once wandered the desert. The trials and dangers faced in the desert were still the same trials they were facing today.

While the Jews were at Rephidim, after being supplied with water, their enemy, Amalek, was prepared to attack. Had Amalek been successful in the battle, they would have killed all the Jewish men and taken their women and possessions, and that would have been the end of the Jewish people. Jesus replayed this story in his mind. It took him back to a more innocent time in his life, his youth. He used to love to sit and listen to the stories of his ancestors. He would ask his mother and father to tell him these stories over and over. They were stories of triumph and courage, stories of faith and fellowship with God. They brought happiness to him. So even here, hanging on the cross, his body beaten and bleeding, he found his mind drifting to these stories of old.

Amalek came and waged war against Israel in Rephidim. So Moses said to Joshua, "Choose some men for us, and tomorrow go out and engage Amalek in battle. I will be standing on top of the hill with the staff of God in my hand." Joshua did as Moses told him: he engaged Amalek in battle while Moses, Aaron, and Hur climbed to the top of the hill. As long as Moses kept his hands raised up, Israel had the better of the fight, but when he let his hands rest, Amalek had the better of the fight. Moses' hands, however, grew tired; so they took a rock and

put it under him and he sat on it. Meanwhile Aaron and Hur supported his
hands, one on one side and one on the other, so that his hands remained steady
until sunset. And Joshua defeated Amalek and his people with the sword.

—Exodus 17:8–13

A man of great faith had led the triumph that day. If Moses held his hands outstretched to God in praise, Israel could win the fight. Jesus looked at himself hanging on the cross, and the wonder of God's great plan became so evident to him. Israel would not have survived if Moses had not stayed in a constant state of praise to the Father. Nor would salvation be found for anyone now if Jesus did not remain in a constant state of praise. This cross on which he hung took on a new meaning for him. He realized that by being nailed to this cross, his hands were outstretched to God in praise of the heavenly Father. His hands would be supported by these nails and never tire or have to be put down. In this way, those he cherished deeply would be strengthened in their struggle against evil. Though he knew it would bring him intense suffering, Jesus embraced his role willingly, drawing profound solace from the knowledge that his sacrifice would empower them. Through every moment of pain, he continued to offer glory to God, finding purpose in each heartbeat of suffering as an act of unwavering love and devotion. In his wonderful and beautiful plan, forever, Jesus would be symbolized as hanging on the cross—not in a state of pain, defeat, or humiliation, but in triumph over death. Forever, he would have his hands stretched out to God for his glory and for the salvation of the people he loved so much. Jesus' heart welled up with emotion, and the thought of being nailed to the cross now brought joy to his heart. As he had discovered on his way here while carrying the cross, the cross represented truth and freedom. The reality was that humanity, frail and burdened by sin, struggled in its weakness. Jesus had now become one with this truth, bound to it in a profound unity that could never be undone. Jesus would now and forever be the symbol of that faith.

Jesus looked over at his hand and desperately wanted to touch the nail that held it in place. The attempt to close his hand around the nail was futile; the only thing he could do was get one finger in contact with the head of the nail. The pain of moving his hands in this manner was immense, but Jesus didn't care at this point. His fingertip touched one of the nails that pierced his body. The nails he had cursed as they drove through his flesh, he now revered. These nails, like Aaron and Hur, would support Jesus' hands for eternity, keeping them stretched out to heaven. These sharp and cold pieces of metal would be the thing that separated man's defeat from Jesus' victory. He understood the nails now. They represented desire.

People longed for a better life. They longed for love, peace, and prosperity. Jesus knew people were good at heart and wanted to be faithful to God. He understood that their pursuits were rooted in the tangible, drawn to the fleeting fulfillment of material gain—things they could hold, claim, and control. In earthly acquisitions, humanity found a semblance of purpose, a fleeting satisfaction. Yet, Jesus yearned for them to grasp salvation, an eternal treasure that no hand could seize alone. He recognized that this higher path eluded man by his own striving. It was human desire, unyielding and blind, that had fixed the Redeemer to the cross of divine truth, their longing becoming the very nails in his hands. Jesus and the cross would be one now for God's glory. The cross of truth, the desires of men, and the Savior could now never be separated. Like the Father, the Son, and the Holy Spirit could not be separated, these three would be bound for all time. Jesus was glad to be the common link between these two trinities. Here, on this day, man had been brought one step closer to God. A New Covenant had been established for the salvation of souls in heaven, which was what God had wanted all along.

As Jesus opened his eyes, he looked down at the people he loved so much. Something had changed for him. He saw everyone differently than before. He could see their faith shining like lamps in a darkened room. Their figures seemed to be out of focus, but the light inside them shone through the darkness with radiance and grandeur. He could not really make out the faces, but there was no mistaking who was who. He saw his beloved mother, and he knew it was her, for her light shone brighter than anyone else's. Jesus could discern the guards among the crowd with ease; their presence was shrouded in an almost complete absence of light. Their faith, barely a flicker, cast a dim aura that reflected a spirit untouched by grace, a darkness where belief struggled to breathe. However, Jesus could still see the spark of God in them, even if they didn't know it existed. Because of it, he loved them, too.

Jesus became conscious of the fact that he was starting to transform from the flesh into the Spirit. He did not think he would be here in this place much longer. His eyes were looking at the world in an unusual way, and his soul was transforming, but the pain and exhaustion were still with him. He had done what the Father had sent him to do, and now he was prepared to move on. He had seen the wisdom and glory of God, and he had graciously accepted this torment for obedience's sake and for the salvation of man. Jesus hung there in agony and patiently waited. He kept watch for angels, thinking God might send them to aid him in his death, but none came. Jesus was tired of the pain. The excruciating pain in his hands and feet was more than he could bear. His insides felt as if they were swelling, and they hurt more than ever. It had grown to the point that there was no more room for his organs, and the pressure made his every breath very shallow. His shoulders were weary from supporting his body's weight, and his muscles burned from fatigue. His head was spinning, and his eyes could no longer focus. The pain from the thorny crown, mixed with the stress of the situation, made him wish he could just pass out or that the Father would relieve him of this suffering.

Jesus continued to wait with faith—but where was God? He wondered why he was still hanging on the cross. God knew he was ready to pass, but he did not come to receive Jesus' spirit. As Jesus hung there for what seemed like hours, despair began to set in. He did not understand why he was made to suffer for so long, and he was at the point that he just wanted to die. He knew nothing could stop his body from dying, and he was ready. The pain was so immense, and he had suffered so much. His mind became dark, and he could not see the light of day—or the light of the faith. He felt alone and abandoned. He became sad and desperate. Sorrow filled his soul—not just because of the suffering, but because he had been so faithful and now felt abandoned. He had done all that was asked of him, including enduring torture and crucifixion.

Have I not done enough yet? Jesus wondered. Why doesn't Abba hear me? Thoughts such as these filled his mind. Jesus had never felt this alone before, but now, in his most desperate hour, he found himself in the pit of utter despair. It was more than he could take.

At three o'clock Jesus cried out in a loud voice "Eloi, Eloi, lema sabachthani?" which is translated, "My God, my God, why have you forsaken me?"

—Mark 15:34

Jesus tried to raise his head to look toward heaven, but he found it impossible. His neck no longer had the strength to lift his head that high. He strained to look for the Father, but he saw something else. In the distance, along the horizon, he saw the Ark of the Covenant descending to the earth; it became one with his mother, and then it rose back up into heaven. The vision was clear and bright to the point of being blinding. It was a wonderful and glorious vision that Jesus pondered in his mind for a few moments. He knew it was from Abba, and a sense of calm came upon him. He hadn't been forgotten or ignored. Once again, despite his condition, he found himself at peace. He immediately understood the vision. His blessed mother, Mary, was the new Ark. The old vessel had carried God's laws, and the new Ark—this beautiful woman, Mary—had carried the perfection of God's Law in her womb. Jesus' purpose was to simplify and perfect the Law. Jesus' mission was clear—to reveal to every soul the profound truth that they were created for a singular purpose: to embody and fulfill God's perfect love.

Jesus continued to watch as the Ark rose. As the old Ark was a vessel meant to hold the laws of God, a burden to be carried by the people, Jesus was meant to carry the truth that men are sinners, but he would forever shoulder this burden for them. This was the New Covenant with God. Without this transformation, salvation for man would be lost. As Jesus looked back toward the vision, he saw heaven open up and all bow to the rising Ark. He knew what this meant. The Father would exalt his loving mother as a queen in heaven. This thought brought Jesus peace. His heart had been breaking for her, even though he had placed her with John, who would make sure she was well cared for.

Jesus was the faithful son of his heavenly Father and his earthly mother. In his heart, Jesus found solace in the promise that he and his mother would be glorified by God, knowing that their sacrifices would be honored in eternity, lifting both of them beyond the bounds of suffering into everlasting grace. This beautiful woman who had cared for Jesus here on earth would be loved and cared for by the Father in heaven. Jesus would not have to worry about her or her well-being. He knew through the vision of the rising Ark that Mary would be blessed for all time. He prayed that all people would come to know and love her the way he did. She was a compassionate mother filled with the grace and love of God.

Though Jesus knew he would soon be reunited with those he loved, a quiet ache still lingered in his heart at the thought of leaving them. Yet, he felt the divine call pressing him forward—it was time to move on, time to fulfill the purpose for which he was sent. He understood, and he was thankful the Father had not abandoned him on the cross after all. The decision to pass on had always been his. God had denied nothing to his beloved and faithful son. He was just waiting for Jesus to let go of the world and those whom he loved so much. This was the only way Jesus could embrace his true nature. Jesus realized that he had held on to his humanity tightly and that his inner self had considered it to be very precious. He understood why people put so much effort into identifying with their human side. God had made man in such a wonderful and glorious manner that it was nothing less than miraculous to be human. People were, without a doubt, the greatest of all God's creations. Jesus became conscious of the fact that humans were born with the ability to create and love, just like the Father. In this final moment, Jesus felt a profound kinship with humanity, realizing that even after a life among them, the depth of the human experience—their struggles, doubts, and pain—had only fully revealed itself in his own suffering and sacrifice. It was in his final breaths that he truly grasped the gravity of what it meant to be human.

At this final hour, it felt less like an ending and more like the dawning of something eternal and profound—a beginning that would resonate through all ages. At the end of his earthly life, Jesus found the true grace of God's wisdom. It was not in denying humanity where God was found. It was only by embracing both the best of humanity and the Spirit that one could have complete access to the Kingdom of God. Jesus realized that humans needed to deny their desire to sin and allow the Spirit to be their internal light. But once that happened, they would need to join humanity and Spirit together in the soul to be complete. That's what Jesus was now— complete. He was ready to let go of the earth and join his Father in heaven. He wished all people could see this moment, understand its significance, and follow His example. Jesus had finally let go of the fear, the pain, the suffering, and the guilt he felt at leaving his mother. The longing he had for his friends and those he loved was now a blessing instead of a curse. He was free from exhaustion, but most of all, he had let go of his sorrow. These were things of the flesh, and they had kept him on the cross. Now, Jesus was no longer just of the flesh. He had transformed into something much more, something he wished all people to have. He embraced the light of God, and through his trials and his faith, he became one with the Father. He was patient, kind, and never jealous. He was poor and humble, never boasting of himself, always giving credit to God the Father. He was neither rude nor quick-tempered, and he refused to give credence to his own self-interest. He forgave everyone for all they had done to him, including nailing his body to the cross to die.

Jesus is the truth, the way, and the life. He carried the weight of all burdens, enduring every sorrow and suffering for the redemption and hope of humankind. He believed in all things from God, hoped in all things from God, and endured all things for the glory of God. Jesus knew the Father's love never failed.

Jesus prayed for everyone as this wave of grace came upon him. He prayed that all would embrace the Holy Spirit and complete their humanity by uniting with the Spirit for the glory of God. Jesus remembered telling his disciples to "follow me." At that time, Jesus did not know where the Father would send him. However, he knew that through faith and love, God would call him home. In his final moments, Jesus prayed that each soul would find the courage to lift their own cross, bearing it with faith, and follow the path he had paved, leading them homeward to the Father. He would go before each of us to open the gate and prepare for us a place to spend eternity with him.

Though battered and broken, Jesus's body seemed beyond pain, numbed by the weight of suffering. His breaths grew shallow, each one a struggle against the weakness that kept him pinned, unable to lift himself for the air his lungs so desperately craved. But even in his deplorable condition, Jesus felt the peace of the Holy Spirit come upon him. The world had somehow become dark, and heaven's light was all he could clearly see. He was happy to close his mind to the world and just let go. He gave all things to the Father, including his soul and the last breath of his earthly life.

After this, aware that everything was now finished, in order that the scripture might be fulfilled, Jesus said, "I thirst." There was a vessel filled with common wine. So they put a sponge soaked in wine on a sprig of hyssop and put it up to his mouth. When Jesus had taken the wine, he said, "It is finished."

–John 19:28–30

"If you are what you should be, you will set the whole world on fire."

—St. Catherine of Siena

About the Author

Phillip Brescia is a debut author whose deep-rooted faith and gift for storytelling converge in his compelling work, A Path of Sorrows. Drawing from his own turbulent spiritual journey and decades of living with undiagnosed depression, Phillip delivers a profound and intimate retelling of Christ's passion from a first-person perspective. His search for understanding life's pain and sorrow led him to an unexpected revelation: that our greatest struggles often pave the way to discovering our Divine purpose.

A construction project manager by day, Phillip finds joy in leading a vibrant youth mission team, traveling abroad, serving others, and savoring good food. His passion for helping others see beyond life's challenges drives his work, inspiring readers to embrace their trials as stepping-stones toward true joy and fulfillment. With A Path of Sorrows, Phil invites you to embark on a transformative journey that reveals the hidden beauty in life's hardships—and the profound purpose they hold. He is dedicated to guiding others on the path to uncovering their Divine purpose and experiencing the profound joy that comes with it.

www.ingramcontent.com/pod-product-compliance
Lightning Source LLC
Chambersburg PA
CBHW071519120626
46550CB00006B/2282